# FIELD & STREAM

# SHOTGUN GUIDE

## SHOTGUN SKILLS YOU NEED

# FIELD & STREAM

# SHOTGUN GUIDE

## *SHOTGUN SKILLS YOU NEED*

**PHIL BOURJAILY**
**AND THE EDITORS OF *FIELD & STREAM***

weldon**owen**

# CONTENTS

# 01 FOLLOW THE BASIC SAFETY RULES

If you've been shooting for any time at all and had any kind of proper education (by which we mean anything from a firearms certification class to a big brother who slapped you upside the head for acting stupid), you should know these rules. We're reminding you here because it never hurts to be reminded and because reading it together is a great starting point for a discussion about safety with a kid or any other new shooter.

**ASSUME EVERY GUN IS LOADED** Every time you see a gun, pick up a gun, or point a gun, always assume that it's loaded, and treat it accordingly.

**CARRY SAFELY** Make sure your safety is always on and that the barrel is pointing down when you are walking with or transporting your gun. The one exception is when you're hunting with a dog; for more info, have a look at item 59.

**BE SURE OF YOUR TARGET** Be absolutely sure that you are shooting at an animal and not a human, and that no people are anywhere near the animal you are shooting at. Never shoot at just a sound or movement.

**DRESS RIGHT** Wear at least the required amount of orange so that you don't become another hunter's target.

**CONFIRM YOUR KILL** Make sure all animals are dead before you put them in or strap them onto your vehicle.

**BE KID SMART** Do not bring small children with you hunting. Wait until your kids are old enough to understand and follow all of these rules before you bring them hunting.

**CLIMB CAREFULLY** Do not climb up or down a tree or over a fence or any other obstacle with a loaded gun.

**KEEP YOUR FINGER CLEAR** Make sure your finger stays off the trigger until you're ready to shoot.

**SHOOT SOBER** Alcohol and firearms don't mix; it's just plain common sense. Save those beers until the end of the day.

**REMEMBER RANGE** Look well beyond your target before you shoot. High-powered ammunition can travel up to 3 miles and still be deadly.

**BUDDY UP** Hunt with a buddy. If you can't, then at least make sure that someone knows where you will be and a time to expect you back.

**STRAP IN** If you're using a tree stand to hunt, don't forget to wear a safety belt. A lot of hunting injuries involve falling from a tree stand. You really don't want to have to tell the guys at work that's how you broke your arm.

**CHECK IT OUT** Before you begin the hunting season and before you use any new or borrowed equipment, make sure to go over everything and make sure that it is working properly. Make sure you know how everything operates before you attempt to use it while hunting.

**STORE SAFE** Store and transport ammunition separate from your guns. Keep everything secured under lock and key when it's not in use.

#  GET JUNIOR A SHOTGUN

A 20 gauge is by far the best choice for a first shotgun for kids. It's lightweight and slim, and the ammunition still packs enough shot that it's an easy gauge to hit the targets with. The .410 can make hitting the target too hard, and the 28 is too expensive to shoot and limited in nontoxic choices.

**THE CASE FOR A PUMP** Inexpensive pumps are easy for small hands to operate; pulling the bolt handle of many autoloaders requires strength. Moreover, pumps are safer than autos or two-barreled guns once you begin loading more than one shell at a time, as you have to work the action to chamber a second round.

**THE CASE FOR A SEMIAUTO** Lightweight pump shotguns put out a lot of kick. The recoil reduction of a gas semiauto makes it a better choice for kids who'll practice a lot. Loaded with one shell at a time, the semiauto is just as safe as a pump. You'll find that the first time you let kids load all three shells in a semiauto in the field, they'll empty the gun every single time without hitting anything.

**THE CASE FOR A DOUBLE** Any break action has the advantage of safety. It's easy to see when a break action is open and completely incapable of shooting, and you can open it and peek down the bores to be sure they're unobstructed. That said, it also combines the disadvantages of a pump and a semiauto: It has the recoil of the pump and the instant follow-up/ammo-wasting capability of a semiautomatic.

# 03 LEARN THE ANATOMY OF A SHOTGUN

Whole books have been written about the arcane terminology of shotguns (including "chopper lumps," "dolls heads," "water tables," and many more), but here is a quick guide to the important parts—which is to say, the ones that hold the guns together, help us hold on to them, and make them work.

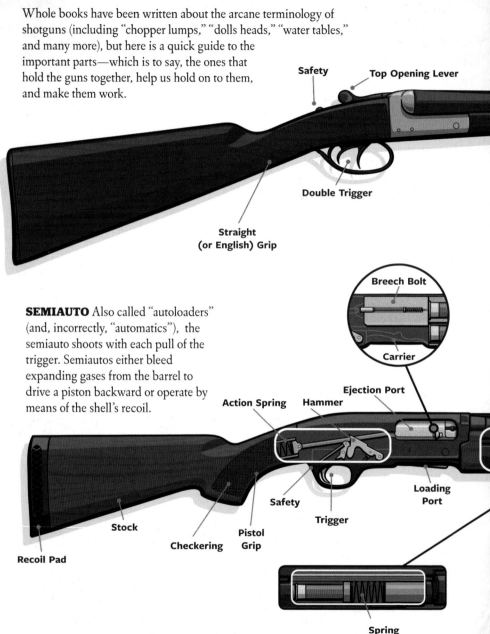

Safety

Top Opening Lever

Double Trigger

Straight (or English) Grip

**SEMIAUTO** Also called "autoloaders" (and, incorrectly, "automatics"), the semiauto shoots with each pull of the trigger. Semiautos either bleed expanding gases from the barrel to drive a piston backward or operate by means of the shell's recoil.

Breech Bolt

Carrier

Ejection Port

Action Spring

Hammer

Loading Port

Safety

Trigger

Stock

Pistol Grip

Checkering

Recoil Pad

Spring

**DOUBLE** Commonly called "side by side," the double has two barrels joined horizontally. Twin triggers, one firing each barrel, are very common on double guns.

Barrel

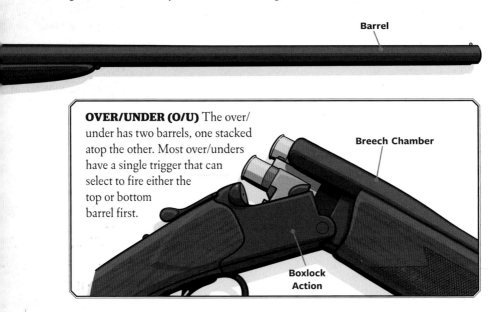

**OVER/UNDER (O/U)** The over/under has two barrels, one stacked atop the other. Most over/unders have a single trigger that can select to fire either the top or bottom barrel first.

Breech Chamber

Boxlock Action

Gas Ports (inside)    Middle Bead    Ventilated Rib    Front Bead

Magazine Cap

Fore-end

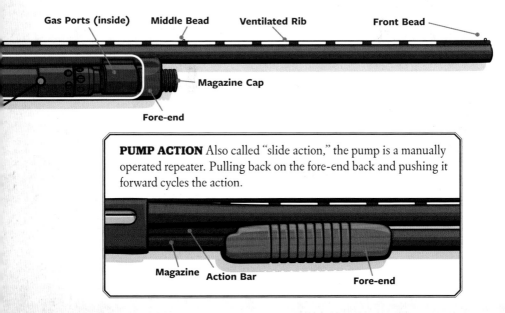

**PUMP ACTION** Also called "slide action," the pump is a manually operated repeater. Pulling back on the fore-end back and pushing it forward cycles the action.

Magazine    Action Bar    Fore-end

 **BUILD YOUR HOME GUN BENCH**

While I leave major jobs to a gunsmith, I like to be able to take guns apart and put them back together, mount scopes, switch stock shims, and so on myself. My gun bench contains the following:

## THE BASICS

- A gun cradle to hold guns so I can work on them with both hands

- A Phillips-head screwdriver for removing recoil pads

- A large flat screwdriver for removing stock bolts

- Mini versions of both flat- and Phillips-head screwdrivers

- A socket wrench with extension for removing stock bolts that don't have slotted heads

- A spanner made for removing pump-action forearms

- A set of roll pin punches

- A set of gunsmithing screwdrivers with interchangeable heads so I don't mar any screws

- Loctite (blue) for scope mounting

- Scope levels

- Allen and Torx wrenches for scope mounting

- Brass/nylon hammer for tapping without denting

- Vise-grip pliers for grabbing things that are really stuck or for holding small parts while I butcher them

- A set of jeweler's screwdrivers for very small screws

- A Leatherman Wave multi-tool, mostly for its needle-nose pliers

- A complete set of hex wrenches

- A trigger-pull scale

### ON MY WISH LIST:

- Brownell's padded magazine cap pliers

- A Hawkeye Bore Scope that connects with a TV screen so I can really get a good look inside a barrel.

### I AM ALWAYS OUT OF:

- Spray cans of compressed air

- Birchwood Casey Gun Scrubber

## CLEANING AND LUBRICATING SUPPLIES

- Cleaning rods with phosphor-bronze brushes and wool mops in all gauges (10-gauge brushes make good 12-gauge chamber brushes)

- Old toothbrush

- Round brushes

- Plastic pick (looks like a dental tool)

- Cotton patches

- Rags

- #0000 grade steel wool

- Shooter's Choice Grease for hinge pins and magazine cap threads

- Birchwood Casey Choke Tube grease

- Gun oil in spray cans and bottles (not WD-40)

- Birchwood Casey Gun Scrubber or Liquid Wrench for thorough action cleanings

- Spray can of powder solvent for bore cleaning

- A box of Q-tips

- A can of lighter fluid for small degreasing jobs

- A bottle of lens cleaner for cleaning scope lenses. Also, lens tissue.

- A jar of Brownell's Action Lube (pretty much the same stuff as choke-tube grease)

- A bottle of clear nail polish for freezing trigger screws in place

- Many jars of J-B Non-Embedding Bore Cleaning Compound

- Shooter's Choice Powder Solvent

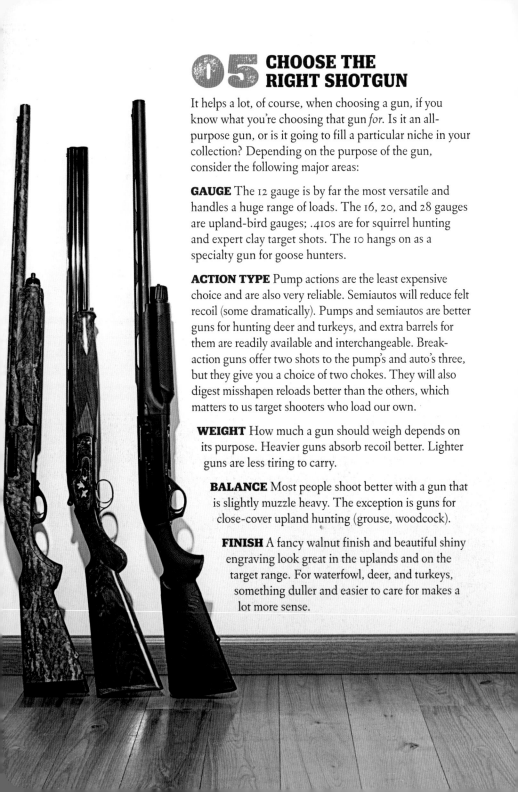

# 05 CHOOSE THE RIGHT SHOTGUN

It helps a lot, of course, when choosing a gun, if you know what you're choosing that gun *for*. Is it an all-purpose gun, or is it going to fill a particular niche in your collection? Depending on the purpose of the gun, consider the following major areas:

**GAUGE** The 12 gauge is by far the most versatile and handles a huge range of loads. The 16, 20, and 28 gauges are upland-bird gauges; .410s are for squirrel hunting and expert clay target shots. The 10 hangs on as a specialty gun for goose hunters.

**ACTION TYPE** Pump actions are the least expensive choice and are also very reliable. Semiautos will reduce felt recoil (some dramatically). Pumps and semiautos are better guns for hunting deer and turkeys, and extra barrels for them are readily available and interchangeable. Break-action guns offer two shots to the pump's and auto's three, but they give you a choice of two chokes. They will also digest misshapen reloads better than the others, which matters to us target shooters who load our own.

**WEIGHT** How much a gun should weigh depends on its purpose. Heavier guns absorb recoil better. Lighter guns are less tiring to carry.

**BALANCE** Most people shoot better with a gun that is slightly muzzle heavy. The exception is guns for close-cover upland hunting (grouse, woodcock).

**FINISH** A fancy walnut finish and beautiful shiny engraving look great in the uplands and on the target range. For waterfowl, deer, and turkeys, something duller and easier to care for makes a lot more sense.

## UNDERSTAND BARREL LENGTH

You will hear that longer barrels "hit harder" than short barrels and that they have a longer sighting plane. Both statements contain an element of truth, but neither is a compelling reason to choose a gun with a longer barrel.

The main reason to choose one barrel length over another is balance. The longer the barrel, the more muzzle-heavy a shotgun feels. And, while we all instantly fall in love with the gun that jumps to our shoulder when we try it at the gun counter, slow and steady usually beats fast and flighty when you're in the field.

For most people, a pump or auto with a 26- or 28-inch barrel, or a double gun with 28-inch barrels, makes the best all-around

field gun. Target guns—even guns for very fast games like international skeet—have 30- and 32-inch barrels, both because the extra weight combats kick and also because it helps smooth your swing on clays that won't change direction as real birds sometimes do.

Longer barrels deliver slightly more velocity than shorter barrels, and, in some cases, they'll give better patterns, as they allow the shot charge time to stabilize in the barrel. The difference is minimal, however. And, while long barrels do offer a longer sighting plane, if you are sighting down your barrel, you're probably going to miss anyway, so it shouldn't be a serious determining factor.

 ## GET BY WITH JUST ONE GUN

One of the first shotgun columns I ever wrote was "The One Gun That Does It All." A friend mentioned he had seen it. I was eager to hear his reaction until he said, "Thanks a lot. My wife read your column, then she asked me: 'Why do you need all these guns? It says here in *Field & Stream* you only need one.'"

While I have learned since then not to talk about it so much in print, it actually is true: You can easily get by with one gun if you must. The trick, of course, is to choose the right one.

The one gun that does everything is an alloy-receivered, 3-inch, 12-gauge, gas semiauto with a 26- or 28-inch barrel. Why? Let's break it down. The alloy receiver keeps the weight light enough to carry

in the uplands, yet the gun will be long enough to be balanced to feel like a heavier gun when you shoot birds or clay targets.

Next, there's the gas action, which will reduce recoil despite the gun's overall light weight, making it a decent gun for skeet, sporting clays, and league trap. Choosing a 3-inch chamber in place of 3½-inch gives you better reliability with very light loads (even near-recoilless ⅞-ounce practice loads). On the other hand, 3-inch waterfowl magnums, turkey loads, and buckshot give up very little in effective range to 3½s.

So yes, you can probably get by with one shotgun. But if you really thought that approach was the right one for you, you wouldn't be reading this book.

**SHOOT A SHEET**

Shooting a bedsheet is a quick and easy way to learn if your gun fits you properly.

Here's what you do: Hang it up, make an aiming mark on it, and measure off 16 yards. From there, start from a gun-down position, mount the gun smoothly, and shoot without hesitation when the butt touches your shoulder. Don't correct if you perceive you're off target, just keep shooting at the mark. After five or six shots, a hole will appear, indicating the average center of all your shots. If the hole is centered over the mark or is an inch or so high, your gun fits you perfectly for field shooting. Every inch off the point of aim will require a $\frac{1}{16}$ of an inch correction to your gunstock's drop or cast, according to gun-fitting theory.

If the point of impact and point of aim differ greatly, roll up the sheet and take it and your gun to a gunsmith.

**TAKE STOCK**

A gun fits when it shoots where you look. The four main dimensions of concern are:

**DROP** The distance from the top of the comb to a line extending back from the rib, drop determines the elevation of your head and eye in relation to the barrel. Drop is usually measured at the heel (the top of the butt) and at the comb (the very front of the comb). Too little drop, and you'll shoot high; too much, and the gun shoots low.

**LENGTH OF PULL (LOP)** is the distance between the front of the trigger and the middle of the buttpad. To some extent, the right length of pull is whatever feels comfortable and maintains about two finger-widths between the back of your thumb and your nose. Changing your LOP can alter drop slightly by shifting the spot at which your cheek meets the slope of the comb.

**PITCH** The angle or pitch of the butt determines how the gun fits against your shoulder pocket. Too little pitch, and the butt digs into your chest; too much, and the gun may slide up and slap your face.

**CAST** A slight lateral bend in the stock that puts the rib in line with the shooter's eye is called cast. Guns for right-handers have cast off; guns for lefties have cast on. In addition, shooters with thin faces need very little cast because their eyes sit above the cheekbone; shooters with round faces need more. Oliver Hardy, for instance, would need a ton of cast. Stan Laurel, not so much.

No Cast · Cast Off · Cast On

## 10 CHECK FIT QUICKLY

Does a gun fit you? A very rough-and-ready way to check is simply to close your eyes, mount the gun, and see if you're looking down the rib. Don't squash your face down on the comb. No one checks the gun as hard in the field as they do when checking fit at the gun shop counter.

## 11 SPACE IT OUT

One more argument for the modern semiauto as the one gun that does everything is the growing inclusion of stock shim kits with most new autoloaders. The shims allow you to fiddle with fit without making permanent changes to the gun. Many guns now come with spacers allowing you to adjust length as well so you can easily experiment with different dimensions.

# 12 TREAT A LADY RIGHT

Just as many women have to struggle with scaled-down versions of men's hunting clothes instead of clothes designed for women, they also have to deal with most "youth and ladies" shotguns being just cut-down men's stocks that ignore the anatomical differences between men and women. Many women have longer necks than men, meaning that a Monte Carlo

Stock (usually seen on trap guns) or a gun with an adjustable pad plate like the Jones Stock Adjuster can provide a better fit.

The toe of a shotgun's stock can dig painfully into a woman's chest as well, so a stock with slightly more pitch and the toe (bottom) of the pad angled outward can give a much more comfortable fit.

Browning Citori White Lightning

# 13 MAKE THE WORST MISTAKE IN SHOTGUNNING

Lord Ripon, the finest shot in Edwardian England, kept his eye sharp in the off-season by potting dragonflies with a .410. The .410 bore has been around since the late 19th century and outsells the 10, 16, and 28 gauges today. It is the only modern shotshell designated by bore diameter. To its haters, the .410 is a crippler and a ballistic disgrace. On the other hand, I know two waterfowling fanatics who shoot geese and swans with .410 handloads. So what is the .410: a toy, a tool, or the worst mistake in shotgunning?

Well, we can start by saying for sure that the .410 isn't a toy. It's a real shotgun, only smaller. That said, despite the light weight of the gun and minimal recoil, the .410 is a poor choice for kids because it is very hard to hit with. There simply isn't room for many pellets inside a shotshell

the diameter of a Sharpie, so the pattern core (the part that smashes targets and folds birds) is smaller in diameter compared to the patterns shot by bigger gauges. There isn't much shot left over to fill out the pattern fringe either.

Twenty-five yards is the .410's effective range. In an unscientific but revealing test, I shot crossing targets with 3-inch hunting loads of 7½ shot. From skeet stations 3, 4, and 5, I could hammer targets at 21 to 22 yards. After I took 10 steps back, I could only crack targets in half or at best break them into three pieces.

Use a .410 within its narrow range of capabilities and it's a proven killer of everything from dragonflies to swans. Stretch that range, and you make the worst mistake in shotgunning: pretending a .410 can do everything a bigger gun can.

# 14 BE A PROUD GIRLIE MAN

A friend of mine came back from northwest Iowa impressed by the numbers of birds but bemused at his reception by the locals. "They called me a girlie-man hunter because I shoot a 12 gauge," he reported. "They said real men shoot 20 gauges."

Me, I do in fact own guns of other gauges, but the half dozen or so that I actually take out of the cabinet to hunt and

shoot with are all 12s. The fact is, no other gauge comes close to being as versatile as the 12 is. Mine range from a double weighing less than most 20 gauges to a near 9-pound target gun with 32-inch barrels, and I shoot loads from $3/4$ of an ounce (for targets) up to $1^3/4$ ounces (for turkeys).

If you shoot steel shot, it takes a hull the size of a 12 gauge's to hold enough of the light pellets to kill a duck or a goose. And, as much fun as light, skinny small bores are to handle, I believe it's easier to shoot well with a gun that's a little more substantial and hand-filling.

All of the above seem like logical reasons to shoot 12s to me. Still, the idea persists among some hunters that small-gauge guns are somehow more sporting and more manly because they give the birds "a chance." (A chance to fly off and die crippled, maybe.) Me, I will stick to my 12 gauges because when I shoot birds with them, they fall dead. If that makes me a girlie man, I'm okay with it.

# 15 GET FAMILIAR WITH SHOTGUN GAUGES

Unlike rifle shooters, who are faced with a bewildering number of calibers, shotgunners are limited to six: 10, 12, 16, 20, and 28 gauges and the .410 bore. Each has its niche, and each has its fans.

**THE 10 (.775)** The largest legal gauge in the United States, the 10 was an all-around gauge in blackpowder days. It hangs on for one purpose: goose hunting. It patterns well with BB and larger steel shot, and its massive 10-pound-plus weight absorbs the recoil of heavy loads.

**THE 12 (.729)** This is the standard and the most versatile gauge of all. The 12 shoots everything from nearly recoilless ¾-ounce practice loads to 2¼-ounce turkey stompers. Ammunition is available everywhere, and the volume of 12 gauge sales keeps prices low. If you own only one gun, it should be a 12.

**THE 16 (.662)** The 16 is an upland classic squeezed ballistically into a tiny, overlapping niche between the 3-inch 20 gauge and the 12. A good 16, built on a true 16- or even 20-gauge frame, is an upland delight, living up to the 16's billing as "carrying like a 20, hitting like a 12."

**THE 20 (.615)** The 20 gauge is a capable upland performer with ⅞ to an ounce of shot. A 3-inch 20 shoots an ounce of steel, which is enough for ducks over decoys. Advances in slugs make 20s the equal of a 12 in a lower-recoil package. A gas-operated 20 gauge is the best starter gun.

**THE 28 (.550)** I have heard the 28 gauge called "the thinking man's 20" but really it's "the .410 for people who want to crush targets and kill birds." At ranges out to 30 to 35 yards, the light-kicking 28's ¾-ounce shot charge hits with authority. I've killed pheasants with 28s, but it's best for smaller birds and short-range clays.

**THE .410 (67 GAUGE)** Although many kids start with a .410 because it is light and has little recoil, the .410's light payloads, poor patterns, and expensive ammo make it a poor choice for kids and better for expert target shooters. The best place for the .410 in the field, in my humble opinion, is in the squirrel woods.

10 Gauge
.775 inch
1½–2¼ OZS

12 Gauge
.729 inch
⅞–2¼ OZS

16 Gauge
.662 inch
¹⁵⁄₁₆–1¼ OZS

20 Gauge
.615 inch
¾–1⁵⁄₁₆ OZS

28 Gauge
.550 inch
⅝–1 OZS

.410
.410 inch
⅜–¹¹⁄₁₆ OZS

# 16 KNOW YOUR SHOTGUN ACTIONS

What shotgun action do you want? Leaving single shots aside for the moment (great for deer, turkeys, and singles trap but not much else), your choices boil down to pump, semiauto, or break action (over/under or side by side).

**PUMP** This is the least expensive, most popular action, in the United States at least. (The rest of the world shuns them.) The pump or slide action cycles a new shell with each pull/push of the forearm. Pumps keep shooting in dusty, dirty, or muddy conditions, and they're easy to clean. While a skilled hand with a pump gun can shoot them almost as fast as a semiauto, working the slide between shots can be distracting, which is one reason you hardly ever see them in the hands of serious target shooters.

**SEMIAUTO** Each pull of the trigger sends a shot downrange. The semiauto has become increasingly popular, although it ranges from slightly more expensive than a pump to four to five times the price of one. Semiautos have the huge advantage of noticeably reducing felt recoil. While modern semiautos are extremely reliable, they still come in third behind pumps and break actions on that count. Gas guns—which tend to reduce recoil more—can be somewhat involved to clean. Inertia guns, which kick slightly harder, are a breeze to maintain.

**BREAK ACTIONS** Two-barreled guns have the advantage of two chokes (and sometimes an instant choice of chokes), and many shotgunners prefer the balance of a break action. You can buy a decent break-action gun for less than the price of a high-end semiauto, but you can also spend the price of a house on one. Because you can clearly see when a gun is open and unloaded, some believe them to be safer than other designs. They are the best choice for reloaders, since they will handle almost any reload and won't fling valuable empty hulls into the long grass.

# 17 CHOOSE YOUR CONFIGURATION

The classic British game gun and the great American doubles were all side by sides, yet today the O/U is the most popular break action. In the United States, the double hangs on only among tradition-minded upland hunters.

The O/U isn't better; it's just different.

The O/U has a more familiar feel in the hands of hunters familiar with pumps and semiautos. Its most-touted advantage is the "single sighting plane" of the O/U—the narrow profile of the top rib and barrels. It is probably true that O/Us can be shot more precisely, especially when firing at crossing targets.

Side by sides tend to be stocked straighter and have lower ribs, which lets you see more barrel when you mount it. When I shoot a side by side, I always feel as though I'm looking up a two-lane road running uphill. I always think, "How can you miss with one of these?" They are great for upland hunting, where most birds you'll see are going to go straightaway or quarter.

# 18 BEWARE THE BREAK ACTION

Break-action fans have a tendency to talk about the advantage of two chokes and of instant barrel selection (only true with double triggers, by the way).

And to all that talk, despite the fact that I am in truth a double-gun shooter, I will simply say, "Whatever."

Purely in terms of results, which is to say birds in the bag, the third shot of a pump or semiauto and, equally important, the speed of reloading are going to beat two shots and two chokes almost every time.

Granted, if you miss a flushing upland bird twice, your chances of hitting it with the third shot are slim. But if you miss twice and stop shooting with a pump or semiauto, when the second bird flushes at your feet, you aren't going to be left standing there with an empty, broken-open gun.

### 1. Purdey Self-Opener
Purdey artisans start with wood and steel and cut away everything that's not a gun, leaving the custom-fitted essence of a shotgun.

### 2. Remington 870 Wingmaster
Introduced as a cost-saving version of the hand-fitted M31, the 870 pump is a triumph of mass production: a gun that is both great and inexpensive.

### 3. Browning Auto 5
So ahead of its time was John Browning's 1903 long-recoil autoloader that it took 50 years for any other American maker to come up with an autoloading design of their own.

### 4. Remington 1100
The 1100 was the first reliable gas gun, and its soft recoil won over American shooters.

### 5. Winchester Model 12
More than 2 million Model 12s rolled out of the Winchester plant, milled and machined to a glorious slickness.

### 6. Browning Superposed
More than any other gun, the Superposed established the O/U on the American shooting scene.

### 7. Westley Richards & Co. Droplock

Westley Richards introduced the idea of internal hammers cocked by the opening of barrels; doubles as we know them wouldn't be possible without that idea.

### 8. Beretta 390

Beretta's 300-series semiautos set the world standard for gas-gun reliability.

### 9. Perazzi M Series

Perazzis made their name grinding clay in competition, but their gorgeous O/U game guns work just as well on feathers.

### 10. Benelli Super Black Eagle

This is the first semiauto chambered for 3$\frac{1}{2}$-inch shells, and the flagship of Benelli's inertia line of guns famous for shooting every time, no matter what.

### 11. Beretta 680 Series

Along with Browning's Citori, the 680s set the standard of the affordable O/U excellence.

### 12. Parker Double

America's iconic double, "Old Reliable" came in more gauges, sizes, and grades than any other American gun.

### 13. A. H. Fox

Brilliantly simple in design, the American-made Fox was the choice of Teddy Roosevelt, among others.

### 14. Krieghoff K-80

Remington's Model 32 O/U failed in the Depression but was resurrected by Germany's Krieghoff to become one of the world's winningest target guns.

## 20

# KNOW WHAT IT'S WORTH

Anyone interested in used guns should invest annually in a copy of S. P. Fjestad's *Blue Book of Gun Values*. It's the Bible of used-gun prices.

## 21 FIND A BARGAIN

Used shotguns are bargains. Let someone else take the depreciation hit, and you get a gun that will still last a lifetime. Some people shy away in the belief that there is something wrong with any used gun, but shooters get rid of perfectly good guns for all kinds of reasons. They trade up. They need money. (As someone who sold three perfectly good guns to pay for my German shorthair's emergency surgery, I know that's true.) They quit shooting, or they just want a different gun. Most of my favorite guns were bought used. The way I look at it, I'm not only saving money, but I'm also sparing myself the trauma of putting the first scratch on a pristine stock.

## 22 BUY LONG-DISTANCE

Many reputable dealers sell guns long-distance. If you're looking for a particular gun, it makes sense to widen your search by looking online. After you have the gun sent to a Federal Firearms License holder, traditionally there is a three-day inspection period. You should be able to test fire the gun unless it's an unfired collectible, but clarify this with the seller. Be sure the gun is exactly what you want. The gun may be exactly as represented, but if it doesn't feel right, or the wood looks different, or anything else feels off, you shouldn't buy it.

# 23 EVALUATE A USED SHOTGUN

Most reputable dealers will guarantee guns to be free of mechanical defects, but the fact is you still buy used guns "as is." You need to be an informed shopper, so here are some things to look for.

**MAKE SURE CHOKE TUBES COME OUT** Rusted-in or stuck chokes can cost a couple hundred dollars to remove and are a sign the gun has been neglected.

**LOOK DOWN THE BORES FOR PITTING** You might decide to live with very light pitting or have it polished out, but deep pits are deal breakers.

**MAKE SURE THE BARRELS ARE FLUID STEEL, NOT DAMASCUS** To identify Damascus steel, look for swirl patterns or the stamped words "twist," "laminated," or "Damascus." Unless you're an expert in metals, stay away.

**LOOK FOR SAFE SCARS** The toe of the stock can bang into the bottom of a safe, and the receiver's sides can be marred by the bolt handle of a neighboring gun.

**INSPECT BARRELS FOR DENTS** Dents are dangerous but can be fixed. Bulges are very dangerous and also tend to be very expensive to repair.

**LOOK WHERE WOOD MEETS METAL** Wood that is flush with the metal or below its level means the gun has probably been refinished.

**RING THE BARRELS** Take the gun apart and hang the barrels on your finger from the underbolt or forearm hook. When you thwack them, you should hear a clear, bell-like tone. A "thunk" means side or top ribs need resoldering.

**LOOK FOR CRACKS** Check around the tang, the head of the stock, the wrist, and the forearm. Any cracks should be repaired before you shoot the gun.

**CHECK THE STOCK DIMENSIONS** Many older guns, especially American doubles, have lots of drop, making them very difficult to shoot well. A new stock will cost you a few thousand.

**TAKE PUMPS AND AUTOS APART** If the magazine cap is rusted on, the insides are probably neglected. Look for rust or missing rings on semiautos, underneath the forearm.

**CHECK THE SCREWS** Buggered slots mean an amateur has been poking around inside the gun. Also, engraved screws on higher-end guns are expensive to replace.

**CHECK FOR WEAR BY LOOKING AT A DOUBLE GUN'S LEVER** On new guns, the lever angles to the right and gradually moves to six o'clock. If it's past that point, it's time to tighten the action.

**BRING SNAP CAPS AND TRY THE TRIGGER** If the trigger's heavy, deduct the price of a trigger job (usually under $100). For an older double, the price of trigger work goes up to a deal-breaking amount. Make sure the ejectors work, too.

**WIGGLE THE BARRELS** If the barrels wiggle with the fore-end off, the action needs tightening, which costs a couple hundred bucks.

**CHECK CHAMBER LENGTH** Chamber length should be stamped on the barrel. Chambers may be shorter than standard, especially on older 16 gauges. On many guns, the chambers can be lengthened.

# 24 BUILD A $10,000 SHOTGUN

A $10,000 target gun won't break four times as many birds as the garden-variety $2,500 Citori or Beretta 687. Serious target shooters will gladly spend the extra money anyway, hoping it may buy them one or two targets on the margin, which is to say the difference between winning and losing.

An expert once explained the distinction between the 687 or Citori and a high-end gun: "It's the difference between a Corvette and a Ferrari. One is made to be a good car at a certain price; the other is made without cutting corners to be the best there is."

And, of course, a new gun won't automatically turn you into a champion shooter. "A good driver in a Corvette beats a bad driver in a Ferrari," he said "But, take two drivers of equal ability, and the Ferrari wins."

High-end guns also are built to withstand the pounding of shooting hundreds of thousands of rounds. One expert I know has a Perazzi MX 8 that has over 1 million rounds through it. Below is an item-by-item accounting of where your money goes when you buy a base-model, high-end gun like this Krieghoff K-80 (MSRP $10,600).

*Krieghoff K-80*

**WOOD** The wood is straight-grained, strong walnut. The stocks are carefully fitted to be interchangeable. Standard wood like this runs $1,500. You can get AAA walnut, but it's an upgrade.

**STEEL** Target guns use a high-grade steel for performance and longevity. This is Austrian Böhler steel, which is much more expensive than the chrome-moly steel used in most guns' construction.

**BARRELS** Regulating the barrels of an O/U is done today as it was 100 years ago—on a jig that lets a worker fit the barrels to the monoblock. It may take 2 to 3 hours of labor at European metalworkers' union wages to get a set of Krieghoff barrels just right. Every gun is test fired to check point of impact at the factory. Between the cost of the steel and the labor, a set of barrels sells for $3,200 to $4,000.

**RECEIVER** The receiver, the heart of the gun, is engineered for strength and made of tool-grade steel. The sliding top-latch action of the Krieghoff is very strong, and it adjusts for wear. The receiver is made precisely enough that it readily accepts other barrels with little if any fitting. Again, you don't get much decoration because this is the base model. Want gold ducks and deep engraving? Krieghoff engravers can do it, but it adds thousands to the price. A plain receiver and fore-end iron will sell for about $5,900.

**TRIGGER** Target shooters obsess over crisp, clean, reliable triggers. A trigger that malfunctions can cost you a target. So can a draggy pull. It takes time, money and skilled employees to make sure the trigger pulls are good and the mechanism won't fail in competition.

# 25

## SPLURGE ON A CUSTOM SHOTGUN

The world's most famous custom shotguns—London's best guns like Purdey or Holland & Holland—cost upward of $100,000 and take more than a year to deliver. However, custom guns aren't only the toys of the rich. For a small fraction of the price of a Purdey, you can order a gun stocked to your measurements, with your choice of grip, barrel length, recoil pad, and decoration. It will be one of a kind and perfectly tailored to you and the type of shooting you do.

Several makers of hunting and target guns have custom shops. Most allow you to choose among a range of options, including stock dimensions, and your order is typically delivered within a couple of months. For instance, when I ordered a Caesar Geurni O/U, I had it stocked to my measurements and splurged on a classy leather-covered recoil pad. The extras added $1,400 to the base price but made a gun that is mine alone, and looks as good as it shoots.

## 26 ADD THE PERSONAL TOUCH

Personalizing a gun with engraving can cost as little as $400–$500 or as much as you want. The United States has a thriving cottage industry of highly skilled firearms engravers. The best place to see their work is at the annual Firearms Engravers Guild of America (FEGA) show held in Reno, Nevada, every January.

Some customers specify the design, others give the artist free rein. Engraver Lee Griffiths of Hyde Park, Utah, who has engraved spiders and dragons on shotguns at customers' requests, says the rule of thumb is to spend no more on engraving than a gun is worth, although that rule seems made to be broken. For instance, "optimizing" or upgrading old American doubles is a popular custom-gun trend. Says Griffiths: "Usually the gun is a lower grade to start with because the high grades have collector value in themselves."

Not every engraved gun winds up as a display piece. Griffiths recalls doing an elaborate and expensive engraving of a quail hunting scene on a shotgun for a man in Texas. Later Griffiths called and asked if he could borrow the gun back to display at the FEGA show. The man said no. Griffiths said: "I understand." The man said: "No you don't. I can't let you have it right now. It's quail season, and I'm hunting with that gun every weekend."

# 27 SHOTGUN OLD SCHOOL

The nostalgia, challenge, and allure of shooting and hunting with guns like the ones our great-grandfathers used attracts some people to the idea of black powder shotgunning. For these people, a shot at birds isn't complete unless a cloud of sulfurous white smoke billows out of the muzzle in the wake of the wad and pellets. Black powder shotgunning is satisfying, too, if you like playing with components, because every load with a muzzleloader is a handload, assembled in the barrel.

As a rule of thumb, start with equal volumes of powder and shot, meaning you use the same measure for both. By that formula, use 75 grains of FFg powder to $1^1/_8$ ounces of shot in a 12 gauge. That load should generate about 1,000 fps of muzzle velocity, depending on barrel length. Go up or down from there. Consult your manual for maximum loads with modern guns. If you're loading old guns, proceed with caution, and the advice of a knowledgeable gunsmith.

---

**FUNDAMENTALS**

## 28
## LOAD THAT MUZZLELOADER

**STEP ONE** Measure the powder and pour it down the barrel.
**STEP TWO** Add an over-powder wad as a gas seal.
**STEP THREE** Pour in the shot.
**STEP FOUR** Top it with an overshot wad.
**STEP FIVE** Cap the gun.

With double guns, be very careful to load each barrel once, not one barrel twice!

*Thompson/Center Muzzleloader Blued-Realtree*

# 29 TAKE TURKEYS WITH A MUZZLELOADER

Suppose, like me, you find black powder shotguns intriguing, but you hate the idea of having to stop and reload your gun the old-fashioned way after every hit or miss in the field. Simple solution: hunt turkeys. You get all the fun of experimenting with components and working up a load, but you only have to actually shoot your gun in the field once or twice a year.

Another pleasant bonus: black powder guns with choke tubes can deliver turkey patterns rivaling modern guns.

A choke-tubed muzzleloader not only puts XX-Full chokes at your disposal, but because you can remove the choke, you can fit modern plastic shot cups into the muzzle. These cups act as a gas seal, protect the pellets from deformation, and keep the payload together in the barrel, making a huge difference in patterning. The gradual acceleration of slow-burning black powder and the low velocity keep the pellets round in the barrel, and the turkey choke does the rest. I used to load 1 3/4 ounces of 5 shot over 90 grains of Pyrodex in my Knight shotgun and got 90-percent patterns with it. A friend cuts open HEVI-Shot and Winchester Xtended Range shells and loads them in his muzzleloader and gets even better results.

## 30 GO BIG OR GO HOME

Famous 19th-century English sportsman Col. Peter Hawker owned one of the largest muzzleloaders ever: a double-barreled punt gun with 1½-inch bores (roughly a 0.65 gauge!). The gun weighed 193 pounds and was 8 feet 3 inches long. Mounted in the bow of Hawker's gunning punt, the double-barreled gun was used on flocks of sitting ducks and geese when Hawker and his puntsman were able to scull close enough across the tidal flats to make a shot. The gun had to be stood on end to load, and it fired 1¼-pound shot charges over 4 ounces of black powder. It had one percussion lock and one flintlock so that the second shot would be slightly delayed behind the first when both barrels were fired.

Peter Hawker (mounted on Grey) talking to gunsmith Joseph Manton, September 1, 1827

## 31 SHOOT YOUR WAD

Most wads open to release the shot charge as it encounters air resistance. In this configuration, if the wad never released the pellets, they would all fly downrange together in the shot cup like a slug.

Federal's Flitecontrol shell, pictured below, is a notable exception to this standard. In this manufacturer's unique and proprietary shell design, the shot stays in the wad for 15 feet or so out of the muzzle, resulting in noticeably tighter patterns downrange.

This patterning makes this design a great wad for buckshot or turkey loads. Instead of slits, the Flitecontrol wad has vanes that pop out of the sides and open at the rear, functioning as brakes.

# 32

## DISSECT A SHOTSHELL

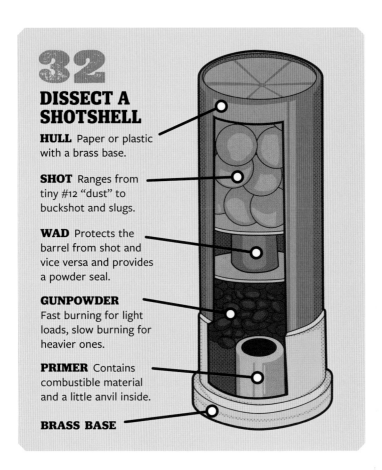

**HULL** Paper or plastic with a brass base.

**SHOT** Ranges from tiny #12 "dust" to buckshot and slugs.

**WAD** Protects the barrel from shot and vice versa and provides a powder seal.

**GUNPOWDER** Fast burning for light loads, slow burning for heavier ones.

**PRIMER** Contains combustible material and a little anvil inside.

**BRASS BASE**

# 33 GET THE BIG PICTURE

Pretty as these pictures are, they don't tell the whole story. Lead shot deforms easily (tungsten-iron and steel, not so much), and the pellets at the rear of a shot column are also subject to deformation. Once squished out of round, they become less aerodynamic, and the added air resistance saps their velocity and sends them off course to become "fliers," which are lost to the main pattern. The best ammunition remedies pellet deformation in three ways:

**BUFFER** Found in premium turkey and buckshot loads, the ground-plastic buffer protects the pellets from each other like foam peanuts do for fragile objects in shipping.

**ANTIMONY** This element is alloyed with lead to harden it. The very best pellets contain up to 6 percent antimony.

**PLATING** Nickel and copper plating doesn't harden pellets, but it does help them flow better through the constriction of the choke.

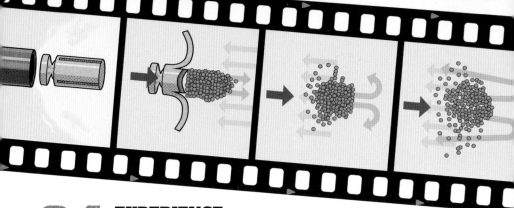

# 34 EXPERIENCE THE BIG BANG

If you were to fire a shotgun in the vacuum of space, the pellets would stay nestled in their shot cup forever as they flew through the inky blackness. Here on Earth, however, atmospheric pressure affects your shot load as soon as it leaves the muzzle on its way to a clay target, a turkey, or a bird in flight.

Hot propellant gases expand suddenly as they exit the muzzle, creating the shock wave that we hear as muzzle blast. In the first 3 feet of travel, air resistance slows the load about 100 fps. The faster you drive pellets through the air, the faster they lose velocity. Increasing velocity by using fast loads does increase energy, but only somewhat. The best way to hit birds harder is to shoot larger, heavier shot.

Air resistance pries open the petals of the shot cup, releasing the pellets. Shot cups protect barrels from hard pellets, such as HEVI-Shot or those made from steel or tungsten-iron. They also prevent soft lead pellets from being deformed by the barrel. A spent cup shows dimples caused by the inertia or "setback" forces that drive the pellets back into the plastic as it accelerates.

Some loads contain a ground-plastic buffer that protects lead pellets at the rear of the shot cup from being crushed by the weight of those at the front, enabling them to retain their round shape and fly truer.

Just 5 feet from the muzzle, the load will already have lost about 150 fps in velocity. As it encounters air resistance, the pattern begins to open up, with the pellets starting to veer off in different directions. The pellets at the back of the pattern are "drafting," like racing cars tucked in behind the leaders of the pack. These trailing pellets will eventually form the central core of the pattern—the dense part with which you hope to hit the target.

The tighter the choke you use, the longer and narrower the shot cluster will be as it leaves the barrel, and the more "drafting" pellets that will remain in the pattern core. The load will also pattern more tightly in thin air than in heavier air due to the lower air resistance. Air is not uniformly dense—it's denser at sea level than at high altitude, and cold air is denser than hot air. The difference may not be much, but it's no coincidence that the record target pattern (most pellets in a 3-inch circle) was shot in the thin air of a hot, dry day. Hedge your bets in the cold, dense air of late season by shooting high-velocity loads or by choosing one size larger shot than you ordinarily would and screwing in a slightly tighter choke.

# 35 CHOOSE SHOT SIZE

Picking a shot size requires you to choose between energy and density. Bigger pellets hit harder, but there are fewer of them in a given weight of shot. Smaller pellets promise multiple hits on the target, albeit with less punch per pellet.

For close-range shooting, smaller shot often proves more effective than larger pellets simply because there are more small pellets in a given shot weight. Out to 30 yards, most reasonably appropriate pellets carry enough energy to kill. The greater number of pellets increases the chances of an immediately lethal strike to the head or neck (a concept very clear to all turkey hunters and some goose hunters). In addition, smaller, more numerous pellets fill out the pattern fringes, adding margin for error if you mispoint the gun. That's why $7\frac{1}{2}$ shot compares poorly in terms of foot-pounds

but, in my experience, hits pheasants hard in the real world at ranges of 30 yards or closer.

The standard advice on shot size, therefore, is to choose the smallest adequate pellet for the job. However, there are times when you don't know at what range the job will have to be done. Pheasants may hold tight or flush wild. Ducks may approach with their feet down or flare at the edge of the decoys. The corollary, contradictory advice to the "smallest adequate pellet" theory is: Under hunting conditions, when ranges are unknown, err on the side of larger shot. Large shot also bucks wind better and plows through dense, cold, late-season air better. As a rule of thumb, a shell containing larger pellets will pattern 4 to 5 percentage points tighter than the next smaller size, too.

# 36 MATCH THE SHOT TO THE BIRD

The following chart gives a quick guideline to shot sizes. The larger sizes in each box should be matched to bigger birds; larger gauges. The smaller sizes are more appropriate for closer ranges; smaller gauges and open chokes.

**Geese**

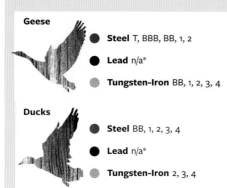

● **Steel** T, BBB, BB, 1, 2

● **Lead** n/a*

● **Tungsten-Iron** BB, 1, 2, 3, 4

**Ducks**

● **Steel** BB, 1, 2, 3, 4

● **Lead** n/a*

● **Tungsten-Iron** 2, 3, 4

**Small Ducks**

● **Steel** 3, 4, 6

● **Lead** n/a*

● **Tungsten-Iron** 4, 6

**Big Birds (Pheasants, etc.)**

● **Steel** 2, 3, 4

● **Lead** 5, 6, 7½

● **Tungsten-Iron** 6

**Medium Birds (Grouse, Partridge)**

● **Steel** 4, 6

● **Lead** 6, 7½, 8

● **Tungsten-Iron** 7½

**Small Birds (Quail, Woodcock, Doves)**

● **Steel** 6, 7

● **Lead** 7½, 8

● **Tungsten-Iron** 7½

*Lead shot is banned from use on migratory waterfowl.

# 37

## MAKE SIZE MATTER

Some hunters swear by a certain shot size. There's something to that, if only because confident shooters shoot well. So if you believe in a particular shot size, it does work better for you. A friend of mine who used to shoot on the high-stakes, high-pressure live pigeon circuit would deliberately mix up the 7½s and 8s in his pouch so he never knew which he was shooting when he practiced. That way, he didn't have a favorite size. "Otherwise," he said, "what if I got to a shoot, and they didn't have my favorite shot size?"

# 38 USE PHIL'S TOP LOADS

You have a lot of options when it comes to picking the best load for various types of game. Here's what I've found to be the best options, through years of experience.

| | SHELL | GAUGE | LOAD |
|---|---|---|---|
| **Pheasants** | 2¾-inch | 12 gauge | 1¼ ounces of 6 shot (lead), 1,300 fps<br><br>1⅛ ounces of 3 shot (steel), 1,500 fps |
| **Ducks** | 3-inch | 12 gauge | 1¼ ounces of 2 shot (steel), 1,450 fps |
| **Geese** | 3-inch | 12 gauge | 1½ ounces of 4 HEVI-Shot (tungsten-iron), 1,400 fps |
| **Turkeys** | 3-inch | 12 gauge | 1¾ ounces of 6 HEVI-Shot (tungsten-iron) |
| | 3-inch | 20 gauge | 1¼ – 1½ ounces of 6 Heavyweight or HEVI-Shot (tungsten-iron), 1,100 fps |
| **Doves** | 2¾-inch | 12 gauge | 1 ounce of 7 shot (steel), 1,300 fps |
| | 2¾-inch | 12 gauge | 1⅛ ounces of 7½ or 8 shot (lead), 1,180 fps |
| | 2¾-inch | 20 gauge | ⅞ ounce of 8 shot (lead), 1,200 fps |
| **Quails** | 2¾-inch | 20 gauge | ⅞ ounce of 8 shot (lead), 1,200 fps |
| **Ruffed Grouse** | 2¾-inch | 20 gauge | ⅞ ounce of 7½ shot (lead), 1,200 fps |
| **Woodcock** | 2¾-inch | 28 gauge | ¾ ounce of 8 shot (lead), 1,200 fps |
| **Deer (rifled barrel)** | 2¾-inch | 20 gauge | sabot slug with premium bullet, 1,500–1,600 fps |
| **Deer (smoothbore)** | 2¾-inch | 12 gauge | 1-ounce slug, wad attached, 1,600 fps |
| **Practice** | 2¾-inch | 12 gauge reloads | ⅞ ounce of 8½ shot (lead), 1,200 fps |

# 39 SPEED IT UP (OR NOT)

The trend in shotshells is higher velocities, both because speed kills and because no one ever got rich selling "slow" to the American public. How important is velocity really?

Velocity improves shotshell performance in two ways: It increases pellet energy, so shot hits harder; and the faster time of flight will reduce the amount of forward allowance (lead) needed to hit your target.

That's the good news. The downside is that increasing velocity increases recoil noticeably. Also, because pellets are round—a poor aerodynamic shape—the faster you drive them, the faster they slow down.

Because of that, you pay a price in much higher recoil for small gains in performance at longer ranges. You might have to endure 50 percent more recoil for a gain of 10 percent in energy and, say, 8 inches less lead needed to hit a crossing target at 40 yards.

The lighter the pellet material is, the more it benefits from high velocity to increase its downrange energy. Therefore steel, which is the lightest shot material, benefits the most from high launch speeds. Lead and denser tungsten-iron pellets, in my opinion, don't benefit nearly as much from added velocity.

# 40 STEEL YOURSELF

If I am often skeptical of the trend toward high velocity, I also believe there are instances when speed does kill. The less dense the pellet material, the more important velocity becomes. Steel shot, therefore, does perform better when you drive it faster, even though it ends up shedding velocity faster than lead and heavier-than-lead pellets.

Early steel loads were slow and the shells were poorly made. The 1990s saw steel improve, and, sometime around 1996, Winchester introduced their black-hulled Supreme loads, with a velocity measured at 1,450 fps. From the first time I shot Supremes, I quit complaining about steel shot and started killing ducks and geese. The combination of a slight increase in energy and a slight reduction in forward allowance really did lead to more birds being hit harder in the front end, thus resulting in quicker, cleaner kills.

I haven't felt the need to shoot faster steel, but I don't want to shoot anything slower, either.

# 41 SHOOT BIGGER SHOT

The best way to increase pellet energy isn't to shoot faster shot. Instead, choose bigger shot. Larger pellets retain velocity better than smaller ones, and their greater mass hits targets harder. For instance, increasing the muzzle velocity of a steel 4 from 1,400 fps to 1,550 results in an increase in energy from 2.22 ft/lbs to 2.48 ft/lbs.

If you're switching from 4 shot to 3 shot at the same 1,400 fps velocity, you increase energy from 2.22 ft/lbs to 3.01 ft/lbs with no increase in recoil. No pain, no gain? Not always.

# 42 LEARN TO RELOAD

Years ago I was in a store with my mother-in-law, who looked at the flies, then the fly-tying materials, and asked, "Why would anyone make their own when they have such nice ones already done up?"

That was my attitude toward shotshell reloading when shells were cheap and my kids weren't old enough to shoot. Now, I roll my own shotshells so I can afford to go to the gun club. And I can make up 7/8- and even 3/4-ounce 12-gauge reloads that have very low recoil, both to soothe my wimpy shoulder and to serve as training loads for new shooters.

Be aware that reloading changes you in ways both good and bad. There's definite pride in shooting homemade ammunition, you can customize your hunting and target loads, there are savings, and looking for hulls adds an exciting little Easter egg hunt to every trip to the range. It is possible to get too fixed on the savings, though, to the point of self-delusion. I once shot with a $100-an-hour consultant who spent what could have been billable time at his reloading bench, putting together loads that saved him 75 cents a box. "Every time I pull the trigger, I'm making money," he bragged. Uh, no. But, you do feel like you're shooting for free when you can reach into a 5-gallon bucket of shells and take as many as you need.

# 43 RELOAD RIGHT

Here's what you'll need to get set up for reloading.

**SOLID WORKBENCH** Emphasis on "solid." Bolt your loader to it to make your loading not only easier but also more consistent.

**RELOADING PRESS** A progressive or single-stage machine for the gauge you will be reloading.

**ACCURATE SCALE** You'll need a scale that can measure up to 2 ounces in grains.

**EXTRA POWDER AND SHOT BUSHING** Most presses come set up to make a basic target load. You may want to make something else.

**COMPONENTS** Shot, powder, wads, primers, and hulls. Buy the first four; scavenge the hulls.

**BROOM AND DUSTPAN** You'll spill powder and shot. Vacuum cleaner sparks don't mix well with powder, and you will want to put any spilled shot back in the bottle.

# 44 CHOOSE YOUR PRESS

Reloading presses come in two basic kinds: the single stage and the progressive. With a single-stage reloader, it takes five pulls of the handle to load each shell.

The difference is in the number of shells produced. A progressive reloader works on 6 to 8 shells at once, with every pull of the handle producing a fully loaded shell for the user.

Single-stage reloaders, on the other hand, produce one shell at a time—as you could probably guess from the name. They are the best option for beginners, not only because they're inexpensive, but also because the process of loading one shell at a time lets you thoroughly learn all the steps of reloading ammunition.

Even so, you can still make a box of shells in 12 to 15 minutes with a single stage. If you only shoot two or three boxes of shells a week in summer trap league to tune up for hunting season, a single stage is all the reloader you'll ever need. A single stage is also best for making smaller batches of custom hunting loads.

Progressive loaders start at twice the price of a decent single stage. They work on several hulls at once, and you can load a box of shells in about 3 minutes. They cost more, and the potential to make bad reloads (no powder, for instance) increases if you don't pay attention.

You will spill more powder and shot with a progressive machine and wreck more hulls. I do, anyway. But, once you get used to the speed of a progressive, especially if you're a target shooter, you'll never go back to a single stage.

# 45 SAVE YOUR PENNIES

Reloading can save you some serious money—up to 50 percent off the high price of factory loads in the small gauges. Here's how to maximize your savings.

**BULK UP** Once you find a load you like, buy components in bulk. A bag of 5,000 wads, a box of 1,000 primers, or an 8-pound bottle of powder offer significant savings over the same components bought in smaller amounts. Most gun clubs pool their buying power for annual buys.

**SEND IN THE CLONES** Claybuster and Downrange produce "clones" of the big three wads that can be substituted for the originals and cost way less.

**GO LIGHT** You save lead when you use less. A 7/8-ounce load yields 102 more shells per 25-pound bag of shot over 1 1/8-ounce shells. Lighter payloads also use less powder.

**SCROUNGE HULLS** Spent hulls on the ground aren't litter; they're money. Look for Remington's Gun Clubs and Sport Loads. You're more likely to find them than the more desirable Winchester AA or Remington STS hulls. Also, when you find target loads with quality hulls on sale, buy them, shoot them up, and reload the empties.

# 46 SEE THE ANATOMY OF A SHOT

Photographs of shot in flight are about as rare as credible photos of Bigfoot. I wrote about the photo that this drawing was made from. It was awesome—and it seems to have been lost to time. The drawing will just have to do.

**THE PATTERN** The duck was a scoter; the range 30 yards. One hundred HEVI-Shot No. 2 pellets from a 3½-inch 12-gauge load containing 131 total hit in the 30-inch circle I drew around the densest part of this pattern. That's a 76 percent pattern. Ideally, your choke-and-load combination should print 70 to 75 percent in the 30-inch circle at the range where you expect to hit birds—15 pellets were about to hit the duck when the photo was taken. Five pellets are usually the minimum needed to kill cleanly.

**THE PATCHES** All patterns have random gaps in them. This example has a couple of big gaps; even so, if you put the duck anywhere inside the circle, multiple pellets will hit it. A pattern that kills effectively in the field doesn't always look so good on paper.

**THE FLIERS** The uncropped photo showed several fliers that had veered out of the main pattern; one in the upper right-hand corner was 4 feet from the pattern's center. Deformed pellets encounter added air resistance that moves them out of the pattern.

**THE SHOT STRING** Some of the pellets look bigger and blurrier than others because they're out of focus. They're trailing behind the main swarm, and they will continue to fall farther behind. By the time this pattern gets out past 40 yards, it may be up to 6 to 8 feet long.

# 47 GET A GRIP ON CHOKE

My first gun was a 12-gauge Auto 5 with a Poly-Choke, an adjustable choke device permanently installed on a gun's muzzle. You twist a collar to open or tighten the choke. Unbeknownst to me, the collar on mine had been removed and put back on by my father, but not all the way, which meant all I was really doing was turning the loose collar and shooting cylinder bore at everything—no choke at all. I killed my first pheasants, ducks, rabbits, woodcocks, snipe, quail, doves, and deer with that gun, raising the question: Are you overchoked? For many hunters, the answer is, "Yes."

Try patterning at 20 yards sometime. Modified, which many regard as an "all-around" constriction, crams almost every pellet of a shot charge into a 16-inch circle at 20 yards. A Cylinder choke at 20 prints a pattern about 25 inches across. Do the math: a 16-inch circle covers 201 square inches; a 25-inch circle spreads pellets across 490 square inches. Which is easier to put on a bird? While a Cylinder choke is deadly at 20 yards, by 30 yards, its patterns spread thin. Since most game birds fall within 25 yards of the muzzle, no choke may be all the choke you'll ever really need.

# 48 PLAY THE PERCENTAGES

Here are the specifications for 12-gauge chokes. Normally smaller gauges require slightly less constriction to achieve tighter patterns. Pattern percentage is for a 30-inch circle at 40 yards.

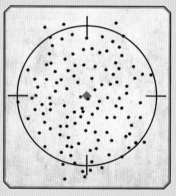

90% on a 30-inch circle at 40 yards

| Choke | Constriction | Pattern Percentage |
|---|---|---|
| Cylinder | (.000–.004) | 40% |
| Improved Cylinder | (.011) | 50% |
| Modified | (.020) | 60% |
| Improved Modified | (.027) | 70% |
| Full | (.036–.040) | 80% |
| XX-Full | (.050–.070) | 90% |

# 49 SIMPLIFY CHOKES

To simplify things almost criminally, a choke functions like the nozzle on a garden hose. When it's open, shot sprays widely; screwed down, the shotshell's load is dispersed in tighter patterns.

Chokes come in thousandths-of-an-inch constrictions (from none at all to .060" or more) and have varying internal geometries. For what it's worth, I have found longer tubes bored with a parallel section before the taper work best. The advent of screw-in chokes in the 1960s means we have so many different choke offerings available that it's possible to become paralyzed by too much choice. Relax. You can get by with just five tubes.

Here's what I'd use. If I had to limit my options, I'd replace Improved Cylinder and Modified with a Light Modified choke.

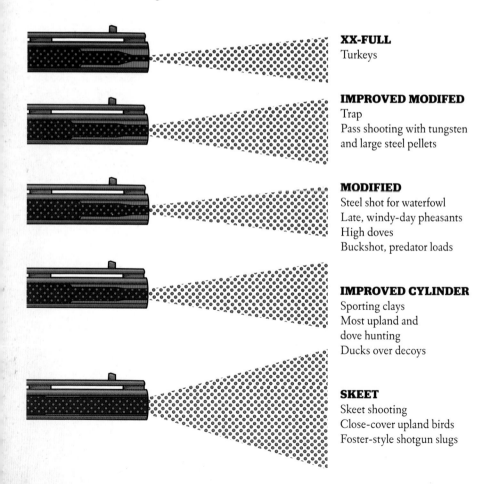

**XX-FULL**
Turkeys

**IMPROVED MODIFED**
Trap
Pass shooting with tungsten
and large steel pellets

**MODIFIED**
Steel shot for waterfowl
Late, windy-day pheasants
High doves
Buckshot, predator loads

**IMPROVED CYLINDER**
Sporting clays
Most upland and
dove hunting
Ducks over decoys

**SKEET**
Skeet shooting
Close-cover upland birds
Foster-style shotgun slugs

# 50 TO BEAD OR NOT TO BEAD

Look at the guns at a sporting clays shoot, and you'll notice something's missing—beads. Many shooters now unscrew their shotgun's bead and throw it away. Removing the bead is a trend that comes and goes. Paradoxically, bright fiber-optic beads are also popular with shooters these days (also with manufacturers, who stick them on "sporting clays" models of other guns, in part to justify the huge price difference). Both types of shooters are trying to keep their eyes from wandering off the target and looking at the muzzle, which is a sure way to miss. When you look at the gun, it stops, and you shoot behind.

You have to know where the barrel is in relation to the bird, but you've got to keep your eye on the bird and the muzzle in your peripheral vision. For some shooters, removing the bead takes away a distraction. For others, it's easier to focus 100 percent on the target if there is a bright bead in their peripheral vision.

So, to bead or not to bead? That is the question. The answer is: whichever method makes it easier for you to avoid looking at the barrel.

# 51 KEEP AN EYE ON YOUR TRIGGER

My trap gun, a Browning BT-100, has one of the niceties of a much more expensive gun: a removable trigger.

Theoretically, if you break a spring in competition you can easily fix it, or take your spare trigger out of the Crown Royal bag you keep it in and be back on the line in a couple of minutes. In reality, coil springs hardly ever break. The reason I like the 100's trigger is that it's jeweled and finely made. I can say, "Hey, check this out," and pop out the trigger and show it to them. I did that for a friend, who told me this story: He was at a gun club on Maryland's Eastern Shore, and one of the shooters in his party had driven a couple hours across the bay from northern Virginia, showing up with a brand new Krieghoff K-80. The guy took the gun out of its case, expecting to bask in the envy his friends. One of them looked at, and said, "Nice gun. Where's the trigger?"

It was at home, safe and sound, in a velvet Crown Royal bag.

# 52 EXPLORE AFTER-MARKET CHOKES

The invention of screw-in chokes has spawned a whole industry in aftermarket choke tubes. Where extended tubes once ruined the lines of a nice gun, now a turkey or target gun doesn't look "cool" without them. Extended choke tubes have three advantages: the longer tubes allow makers to put in a lengthened taper or longer parallel section inside, which can result in a big improvement in patterns over shorter tubes; a longer tube can move the stresses of shooting big, hard, nontoxic shot outside of the muzzle where it's better for your gun; finally, extended tubes are easier to check and change. Before you splurge, pattern the chokes that came with your gun. They might be fine. In my experience, you'll see the most improvement in patterns with aftermarket turkey chokes over factory models, and in general when you replace the shortest factory tubes (the old Winchoke style, still used by Mossberg and some others) with a longer tube. For the very best custom choke results, send your gun to a choke specialist who will measure the bores and make chokes to fit your barrels precisely.

# 53 PAD YOURSELF

Recoil pads are the in thing right now. As guns keep getting lighter, and therefore become harder-kicking, recoil pads get higher-tech and softer. The new pads work much, much better than the hard rubber pads on some guns, and also better than the old honeycombed red and brown rubber pads. That said, manufacturers get a little carried away in the claims for them. Says one: "Our pad makes our pump gun kick less than the competition's semiauto." This statement is simply not true. Take those claims with a grain of salt but put a soft pad on your gun anyway. They are available in both grind-to-fit and pre-fit models for many popular guns.

# 54 BRING FIDO ALONG

A lot of people hunt birds without dogs. I used to. Not anymore. If there are no dogs on an upland hunt, I won't go. Why? Well, if you bring a dog, you'll see more birds on that hunt. You'll kill more, and you'll lose many, many fewer cripples. Beyond that, a dog tells you what's going on in the invisible world of grass and scent under your feet. Without dogs, you're just walking and hoping.

I do hunt waterfowl without a retriever. Many people won't, and they're probably right. Duck hunting without a dog means limiting the shots you take and always being aware of where a bird is going to fall when you make the decision to shoot.

Hunting with a trained retriever means few cripples escape. More than once I've seen a lab dive underwater after submerged ducks and held my breath until the dog broke the surface with the duck in its mouth.

# 55
# GO WITH THE WIND

Dogs hunt with their noses. We all know that. And yet, it never fails to surprise me how many people don't think to take the wind into account when they hunt with a dog. Plan your route so you hit the likeliest cover with the wind in the dog's face. Running a dog downwind is almost like blindfolding him—he's much more likely to bump birds he doesn't smell until he's right on top of them.

# 56 KEEP YOUR EYES UP

When you walk in to a point or approach a very excited flusher, lift your eyes off the ground in front of the dog's nose and up to, well, eye level. If you're looking down, you'll see the bird flush as a blur, and you'll be chasing after it, leading to panic and a rushed shot. When you have your eyes pointed where you want to shoot the bird, you'll be ready to make an unhurried shot.

## 57 POINT OR FLUSH

Pointing and flushing dog owners endlessly argue the relative merits of their relative favorites. Having hunted with both kinds of dog, I'll say it's not as different as either camp would have you believe. I like it when my dogs point birds, but half the pheasants I've killed over them didn't stick around to be pointed. Often, the dog will get birdy, and I'll go on the alert. When the bird flushes through no fault of the dog's, I'm ready, and I shoot it. Because I'm not a pointing-dog purist, I'm happy.

By the same token, flushing dogs don't immediately boost into range every bird they find. Often, when a bird sits tight, the flusher starts rooting around the cover, and you have plenty of time to get to it and get ready. It's almost like shooting a bird over a point.

## 58 BELIEVE THE DOG

"Always believe the dog" is one of the most important rules of bird hunting. My old setter, Ike, and I were once hunting with some friends and a few other dogs. We stopped to rest in the corner of a fence line after a long, birdless walk. Ike went to sleep with his head in my lap. We'd been there a little while when Ike opened his eyes, lifted his head, and sniffed the air. He got up, walked 15 yards, and pointed.

"Ike's got one," I said. No one else believed a pheasant would be stupid enough to stick around for several minutes while we sat and snacked and talked. I didn't really believe it either, but a rule is a rule. I was the only one to stand up, load my gun, and walk over to Ike. A rooster flushed from under his nose. I shot it. Another flushed, and I shot that, too. Those were the only pheasants we saw all day.

#  MUZZLE UP

A while ago, I was hunting grouse with a marine, and after the first time he walked in on a point, I had to tell him that what he had clearly been taught as a safe carry (gun across the body, muzzle pointed at the ground) was all wrong for hunting with bird dogs. Carry that way, and your muzzle sweeps past the dog as you mount the gun. If your finger happens to hit the trigger too soon (I've seen it happen, although fortunately with no dog in the line of fire), you'll shoot your dog. When you hunt with dogs, the muzzle has to be level with the ground at the very least, and preferably angled up in the air. It calms dog owners considerably if you don't point a loaded gun at their best friends.

##  DON'T BE THIS GUY

A friend who used to work for Remington's customer service told me about handling this call.

    Caller: "My 1100 keeps jamming."

    CSR: "Do you clean it?"

    Caller: "Every time I shoot it I clean it just like my daddy taught me. I use a bronze brush and solvent and scrub out the fouling, then run cloth patches through the barrel until they come out clean."

    CSR: "Do you take the forearm off and clean the gas system?"

    Caller: "The forearm comes off?"

# 61

## LINE UP YOUR CLEANING SUPPLIES

I keep the following cleaning and lubricating supplies on hand:

- Bore snakes for when I feel lazy

- Cleaning rods with brass brushes and wool mops in all gauges (10-gauge brushes make good 12-gauge chamber brushes)

- Old toothbrush

- Round brushes

- Plastic pick (looks like a dental tool)

- Shooter's Choice for greasing hinge pins and magazine cap threads

- Birchwood Casey Choke Tube grease

- Gun oil in spray cans and bottles (not WD-40)

- Gun scrubber or Liquid Wrench for thorough action cleanings

- Spray can of powder solvent for bore cleaning

- Cotton patches

- Rags

- Fine steel wool

- Spray cans of compressed air

## 62 CLEAN A SHOTGUN

At a minimum, run a bore snake through the bore and wipe down the outside of the gun with a lightly oiled rag when you come in from the field or range. Use an old toothbrush to get the grit out from behind the ejectors and other hard-to-reach places. If you've been doing a lot of shooting, clean your semiauto's gas piston with a brush and scrub fouling off the magazine tube. Very fine steel wool and a little oil works.

On break-action guns, clean the grime off the breech face and inside the receiver. Remove the fore-end and wipe the barrels.

## 63 GREASE IT WHERE IT NEEDS IT

A light oiling works best for most working parts of the gun, but three spots are better lubed with a dab of grease like the popular Shooter's Choice red grease that comes in a handy syringe applicator.

Grease stays put and does its job on surfaces where oil migrates. Use a dab of grease on the hinge pins and trunnions of a break-action gun. Grease choke-tube threads to keep chokes from sticking in the gun, especially if you shoot a lot of big steel shot. Grease the threads of your magazine cap, too, to keep it from rusting on when a gun gets wet. Use grease sparingly; clean it off and reapply it whenever you clean your gun.

# 64 DO IT QUICK AND DIRTY

I first saw this trick done with Liquid Wrench, and since then, several manufacturers have come up with their own spray-action cleaners. First, you'll need a couple of newspapers. Take the gun outside. Remove the barrel of a pump or semiauto and hold it by the grip pointing down over the papers. Spray the scrubber up into the action. Rivers of crud will run out onto your papers. When it finally runs clear, the action is clean. Oil it lightly and put the gun back together.

# 65 DEEP CLEAN

At the end of hunting season, and after every few thousand rounds shot with target guns, do a full deep cleaning.

First, take your gun completely apart. Soak the piston and other gas system parts of a semiauto in solvent and give them a thorough cleaning.

Next, you'll want to remove the bolts of pumps and semiautos, and then clean all of the parts completely. Use a tiny amount of oil on the firing pin, so that it won't turn sluggish in cold weather.

Remove the trigger group, clean it with a nylon brush, then oil it lightly. Wipe out the inside of the receiver.

On pumps and autos—if it's possible with your particular gun—remove the magazine spring and retainer and clean the spring and the magazine tube with a 10-gauge brush.

You can also remove the stock from a semiauto and remove the return spring for cleaning. It is a pain, but waterfowlers really do need to be sure they take this step.

Start by scrubbing the bores with a bronze brush soaked in solvent, then cotton patches, and then an oiled wool mop.

Use a chamber brush or a 10-gauge bronze brush and solvent on the chamber of 12 gauges to remove plastic buildup. Use a tiny drill bit as a scraper to clean any built-up carbon out of gas ports.

Take out the choke tubes and thoroughly clean them inside and out with a brush dipped in solvent. Brush out the threads in the barrel, too. Then grease the threads and replace the barrel.

A toothbrush works well to clean those hard-to-reach spots beneath and around the vent rib posts.

Break-action guns can go through many thousands of rounds before you have to pull the stock off and lube the locks. If you don't want to do it yourself, take it to a gunsmith.

# 66 BRING THE MOST BASIC REPAIR KIT

One time, I fell down a muddy creek bank on my way to a deer stand. As I flailed, my Browning pump flew like a javelin across the creek and stuck barrel first into the muck. Having no tools with me and several inches of mud packed in the muzzle, I removed the barrel and held it underwater in the icy creek until the current washed it clean. After my fingers thawed, I put the gun back together, loaded it, and shot a deer an hour later. Since then, I've always had with me, or nearby in the truck:

**1.** A bottle of Break Free CLP for loosening sticky firing pins.

**2.** A takedown cleaning rod for clearing out obstructions or punching stuck shells from the chamber.

**3.** A mini Leatherman for punching trigger group pins out (the needle-nose pliers gets them started). I have used the flat-bladed file as an emergency extractor to pry stuck shells out of chambers, too.

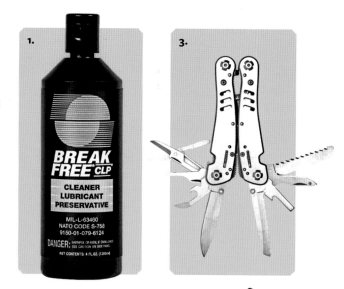

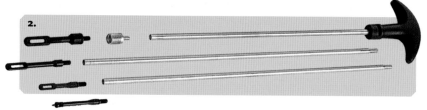

# 67 KNOW THE BEST REPAIR KIT

A friend of mine took a man he didn't know pheasant hunting. As they loaded their guns, the man realized his gun was plugged for ducks. He insisted they stop right there so he could take his gun apart and remove the plug to load five shells instead of three. The magazine spring—as magazine springs will—shot out, taking the spring retainer with it into the tall grass, where they were unable to find it. Fortunately for said hunter, my friend had brought along an extra gun.

# 68 MASTER PRACTICAL PATTERNING

Does your gun shoot straight? Does it shoot too tightly to hit the game you're after? Are your patterns too sparse to kill cleanly? There's only one way to find out: Blast holes in large pieces of paper. A tedious chore under ideal conditions and a paper chase on a gusty day, patterning is still essential homework that must be done. Fooling with flapping sheets of paper, taking aim, and punching holes is no fun; homework rarely is. But, when the final exam comes to you in the form of a greenhead over your decoys, or a quail buzzing into the brush, it's good to know that your shotgun throws enough pellets to fill in the blanks.

**STEP ONE: CHECK POINT OF IMPACT (POI)** Screw in a tight choke and shoot two to three aimed shots from a rest (we want to take gun fit out of this equation) at the same sheet of paper from 25 yards. The center of your shot pattern should have obliterated the aiming point, or a spot 1 or 2 inches above it. Don't worry if you are off target by a couple of inches, but if the POI is far from the point of aim, try a few different choke tubes to see if you have a bad tube. If not, send the gun back to the factory.

**STEP TWO: CHECK YOUR PATTERN** Practical patterning takes place at whatever range you typically shoot your birds. Staple a 40-inch square sheet of paper to a backstop, back away to the appropriate distance, and shoot. Label the target with gun, choke, load, and distance,

put up another piece of paper, trudge back to your gun and shoot at least two more.

At home, draw a 30-inch circle on your sheet with the densest cluster of pellets at the center. You don't have to count the holes; look for a pattern with enough pellets to put four or more hits on the vitals of the species you'll be hunting. Pay closer attention to the 20-inch center, which is the reliable killing and target-smashing part of any pattern. You can make life-size cardboard outlines of game birds and trace around them on the sheet or simply eyeball the pattern.

There will be gaps. There is no such thing as a perfectly even pattern with one pellet strike in every square inch of the circle; shot charges cluster pellets more tightly in the center and spatter them randomly around the edges. If the pattern has many, many gaps in it where only one or two pellets strike the bird, you'll need smaller shot, a heavier shot load, or a tighter choke. Patterns that are overly dense in the center and weak on the fringes will indicate you're using a choke that's too tight.

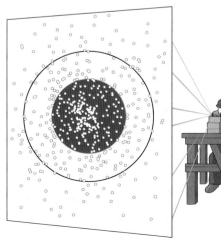

 **LEARN TO SWITCH**

It's much better for a new shooter to learn to shoot from his dominant-eye side, even if it means shooting with his nondominant hand. I taught my older cross-dominant son to shoot left-handed, and he does very well in the field. He's never handled a gun right-handed at all.

The reason to switch sides and be able to shoot with both eyes has nothing to do with depth perception or peripheral vision, in my opinion. It's simply that if you shoot with one eye closed, you see the gun in sharp focus. And the better you see it, the more likely you are to aim it—which is the worst way to shoot a shotgun. Your eye-hand coordination and subconscious mind are much more effective at putting a gun on target than your conscious, aiming mind can ever be. With two eyes, you can "see through" the gun, and it appears as more of a blur, allowing you to keep all your focus on the target, where it belongs.

 **FIND YOUR DOMINANT EYE**

Most people have one eye stronger than the other, just as they're left- or right-handed. While many people have their strong eye and strong hand on the same side, not all shooters do. Cross-dominance is especially common among women. It's very important to ensure your dominant eye is the one looking down the barrel of the gun.

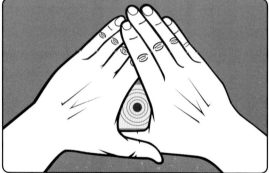

The first thing to do with any beginner is to give them an eye-dominance test. Have them hold their arms straight out, palms outward and overlapping so their thumb webs form a triangular hole.

Tell them to keep both eyes open and look at an object in the distance. Then, keeping that object in sight, have them bring their hands back until they wind up over one eye or the other with the object still in sight. The uncovered eye should be the dominant eye. To be sure, repeat the test, bringing their hands back so they cover the eye you think is dominant. The object they are looking at should be blocked from their view. Watch carefully when you give the test. Some younger shooters will cheat in an effort not to appear cross-dominant. A rare few others will be center-dominant, able to see the object regardless of which eye they cover.

# 71 KNOW WHEN TO SHOOT ONE-EYED

It's not impossible to shoot one-eyed. The great trapshooting champion Nora Ross shoots with one eye shut tight. And, while there's no question that Nora would beat me in a shooting match, think of how much worse she'd beat me with both eyes open.

Nevertheless, some people who have shot on the wrong side for too long can't or won't switch no matter what. Some are center dominant, and if both eyes are equally strong, each eye will take over at different times. These shooters need either to learn to close one eye as they mount the gun or to put a piece of tape on the lens of their glasses to block their dominant eye.

The tape patch can be about the size of your thumbnail. If it's placed just right to block your vision when you mount the gun, it'll be high enough that it won't interfere with your vision when you have your head up normally.

# 72 READY YOUR POSITION

In shotgun shooting, to "assume the position" means starting with proper foot placement and stance and then holding the gun in such a way that it can be brought quickly and smoothly to a firing position. The butt should be tucked very lightly under your arm. The barrel should be parallel to the ground or pointed slightly higher if there are bird dogs in the field with you.

Be sure to keep the muzzle below your line of sight. Your grip should be relaxed, and your finger should not be on the trigger or even inside the trigger guard.

Whenever possible in the field, I'll take a short step toward the target and bring the gun from whatever carry position I'm using into this ready position while my eyes are finding the bird. Then I'm ready to make the shot.

# 73 HIT THE RIGHT BALANCE

You see lots of people lean aggressively forward when shooting a shotgun, back knee locked, front knee bent, or else they lean back, usually a habit formed by trying to handle too long and heavy a gun when they first started learning to shoot.

The proper stance for shooting a shotgun is fairly upright. Your knees are neither bent nor locked, just relaxed. Lean forward slightly, with just over half your weight on your front foot. The easiest way to remember is to think "Nose over toes." When you're standing in the correct position, your nose should be directly above the toes of your front foot.

# 74 COPE WITH A LONGER STOCK

Most shooters can handle a longer gun stock than they're used to if they adjust the placement of their hand on the forearm. It's a simple trick, but it really works. If a stock is too long for you, try taking a shorter grip on the forearm, holding it near the receiver. The shorter grip helps you push the stock out and away as you mount the gun so it doesn't hang up on your clothing. Conversely, if a stock feels too short, try taking a hold out near the end of the forearm, and the gun immediately seems longer. Theoretically, I (at 6 feet tall), Abe Lincoln (6'4"), or Granny Clampett (5'2") all could shoot the same gun just by adjusting our grips.

# 75

## STAND UP FOR YOURSELF

Your feet should be no more than shoulder width apart when you shoot a shotgun. If you were to draw a line from your back heel through your front big toe, it would extend out to the point where you want to shoot the bird or target. Obviously you can set your feet at that angle before you call for a clay target. In the field, taking a short half step toward the spot where you plan to shoot the bird puts your feet in the right alignment.

Stand this way, and you'll put your body in proper relation to the target: halfway between sideways and squared up. Keeping your feet fairly close together lets you pivot easily from the hips and swing in either direction.

# 76

## MOVE THE MUZZLE BELOW THE TARGET

Never let the bird go below your muzzle. To hit a flying target, you have to keep your eye on the bird. If you let the bird dip below your muzzle, you lose sight of it for an instant. Without the target to look at, your eyes can flick back to the bead, the very last place you should be looking. If, on the other hand, you keep the barrel just below the target, the muzzle stays in your peripheral vision as a blurry reference point while you maintain a tight focus on the bird. You see where the muzzle has to go and connect the dots.

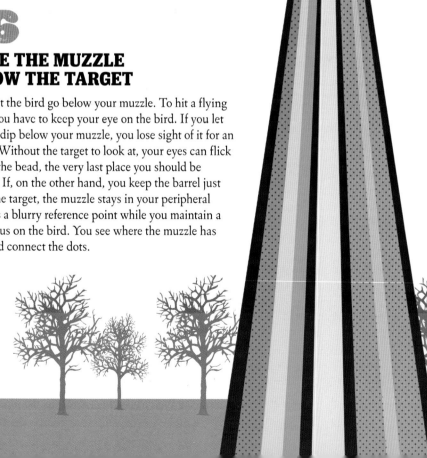

# 77 MOUNT UP

Learning to mount a shotgun is the single most essential skill in field shooting. When you can bring the gun to your face, instead of putting the gun to your shoulder and lowering your face to it, you can look at a target and hit it without hesitation. The gun mount, done properly, combines the swing and the mount as one move, rather than the "mount, find the target, swing, then shoot" method of many American shotgunners weaned on rifle shooting.

Start from the ready position (see item 72). Before you move the gun, you have to see the target clearly so your eyes can tell your hands where the gun has to go, and your head has to come forward and incline slightly to accept the gun. Lock your eyes on the front edge of the target and then begin the mount by moving the muzzle toward the target as if you were going to hip shoot it. As the muzzle flows to the target, raise the stock to your face. The comb nestles under your cheekbone just before you settle the stock into the shoulder pocket below your collarbone. When the gun butt meets your shoulder, pull the trigger.

# 78 SHINE A LIGHT

Practice your gun mount with an unloaded gun and a Mini Maglite in the barrel (AAs can fit 12 gauges; AAAs fit into 20s; sometimes one or two wraps of clear tape make a snugger fit). Do this drill inside, standing in one corner of a darkened room with the beam of the flashlight cranked down to its tightest setting. Hold the gun in a ready position, butt down, with the beam shining into the corner where the opposite walls and ceiling meet.

Mount the gun, raising the stock to your cheek first, and concentrate on keeping the beam from bouncing out of the corner. You only have to do this for a few minutes a night to get results in the field.

# 79

## KEEP IN TIME

When I'm missing a target and don't know why, I try varying my gun speed, which usually means slowing down. A shotgun has to move in time with the target to be effective. I don't completely understand why it's so, but it is. Believe me.

# 80 SWING YOUR SHOOTER

A shotgun is not aimed; it is pointed or swung at the target. A proper swing starts before you begin the mount. The first step is to lock your eyes on the bird. There is no reason to move the gun until your eyes can tell it where to go.

When you can see the target clearly and read its path, move the muzzle toward it as if you're trying to hip shoot the bird. Keep moving—swinging—the muzzle along the line of flight as you raise the stock to your cheek.

The muzzle should stay below the bird so you always have a clear view of the target. Move the gun in time with the bird. I cannot emphasize those two tips enough.

Being too precise with lead will make you slow down or stop the gun and miss, which is why many engineers have trouble shooting shotguns: They want to be exact. Instead of thinking in feet and inches, it helps to think of lead in three increments: some, more, and a lot. "Some" is the amount of lead you see when you shoot a midrange target. "More" is twice that, and "a lot" is twice as much as "more."

The spread of shot provides some margin for error. Trying to aim at the last second practically guarantees a miss. Trust your eye-hand coordination to put the gun in the right place and then just shoot without hesitation.

---

# 81 USE THE RIGHT METHOD

There are two main shooting methods that will get your muzzle in front of a flying target: swing-through and maintained-lead. Most good shooters can switch back and forth between the two as the situation demands.

**Swing-Through** The more intuitive style, swing-through is excellent for upland shooting and short- to midrange waterfowling. Trace the bird's line of flight, shooting as you pass the beak ("butt, belly, beak, bang" is how the British put it). You have to move the gun faster than the bird in order to catch and pass it. Because the gun keeps moving past the bird during the time it takes for you to pull the trigger and the gun to go off, you won't see much apparent lead but the bird will fall.

**Maintained-Lead** The staple method of skeet shooters, maintained-lead is the easiest way to hit long-crossing targets such as doves and waterfowl. Unlike swing-through, whereby you catch the bird from behind, in maintained-lead shooting, you never let the bird pass your gun barrels. Mount the gun ahead of the target, match the bird's speed for an instant, and shoot. Maintained-lead requires longer perceived leads than does swing-through.

# 82
## BAYONET THE STRAIGHTAWAYS

If you want to more easily hit birds that are flushing underfoot and flying off straightaway, just imagine a bayonet on the end of your shotgun. When the bird flushes, take a ready position, with the gun held parallel to the ground just above waist level. Take a short step toward the bird and imagine jabbing it with a bayonet as you bring the stock to your face. Starting the gun low lets you see the bird clearly. Pushing the gun out toward the bird assures you won't catch the butt in your coat. And you should probably skip the part where you scream "Kill!".

# 83 STAY FOCUSED

Ammunition companies will tell you that more velocity solves the problem of missing behind a flying target. Helpful kibitzers at the gun club will tell you that you need to lead the target more or to keep your gun moving. In truth, most misses behind result from the mistake of looking back at the bead to measure lead. It's baffling to experience, because the last thing you saw before you looked at the bead was the gun ahead of the target. However, the instant you look at the bead, the gun stops. You are going to end up shooting behind even though you think you're ahead of the bird. The answer to this problem isn't more feet per second, more feet of lead, or an especially exaggerated follow-through. It's more focus on the target. Relegate the barrel to your peripheral vision and keep your eye on the bird. Think "sharp target, fuzzy barrels," and your mystery misses will quickly turn into solid hits.

# 84 HIT THE HIGH BIRDS

To make long shots on way-up-there birds, move the gun at about half the speed you think you should and shoot as the muzzle passes the beak. Slowing down doesn't seem as if it would work, but it does.

*Remington 870 ShurShot
Synthetic Super Slug*

# 85 GET AN ACCURATE SLUG GUN

**BARREL** Heavy barrel for rigidity and recoil reduction.

**RIFLING** One twist in 34 inches. Slower rates like 1 in 34 usually work best with 1,200–1,500 fps slugs. Faster rates (under 1 in 30) match up with 1,900–2,000 fps slugs.

**PIN** Barrel is fixed to the receiver to dampen vibration. This barrel was pinned at the factory, but a gunsmith can install a set screw in almost any gun to pin the barrel.

**STOCK** High comb suitable for use with optics.

**RECEIVER** Drilled and tapped for optics.

**GAUGE** Get 12 or 20. Twenty-gauge sabots give up little to 12s ballistically and have lower recoil.

**PAD** Soft recoil pad.

**SCOPE** Longer (4 to 6 inches) eye relief for mounting on a shotgun receiver. Low-medium power variable. Heavy reticle to stand out in thick cover.

**TRIGGER** Hard-kicking guns are easier to shoot if they have lighter (between 3 and 4 pounds), crisp triggers. Most factory guns can benefit from a trigger job by a qualified gunsmith.

# 86 CHOKE IT RIGHT

One of the reader questions I get most often is, "Will slugs hurt a full choke gun?" Probably not. The slugs are lead; the barrel is steel. A better question is "Will a Full choke hurt my slugs?" and the answer is "Yes." For instance, a while ago I started with an Improved Cylinder, then switched to Modified and Full in a Mossberg 500 with Federal Truball slugs. IC shot around 3½ inches at 50 yards, Modified did the same, but the Full choke group widened to 7½ inches.

# 87 IDENTIFY SLUGS

**FOSTER SLUG** For smoothbores. The "vanes" don't make it spin, they help it swage down through a choke.

**ATTACHED WAD SLUG** For smoothbores and rifled barrels. The attached wad keeps the slug flying straight, like the feathers on a badminton shuttlecock.

**SABOT SLUG** The halves of the sabot separate and fly off after the round leaves the muzzle. Expensive and worth it in rifled barrels where they are accurate enough to take deer to 150 yards. Very inaccurate in smoothbores.

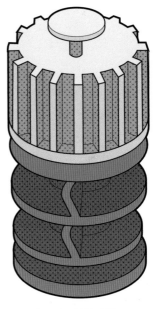

Attached Wad Slug

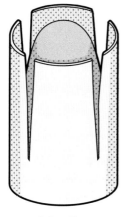

Sabot Slug

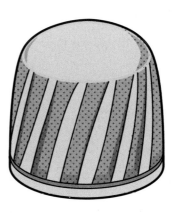

Foster Slug

## 88 GET A GRIP

We all know we're getting kicked when we shoot a slug from the bench. What we don't understand is that slug recoil can play a nasty trick on us. Slugs are so slow that they're still traveling down the barrel as the gun recoils upward and to the left, due to the torque of the heavy projectile as it spins out of the barrel's rifling. If you sight the gun in at the bench without holding the fore-end, you'll actually sight it in 5 to 6 inches high and to the left of where it will shoot when you hold the fore-end normally in the field.

Adjust your benchrest technique. Rather than using your left hand to plump up the sandbag as you would with a centerfire rifle, clutch your gun's forearm firmly or even put your hand on top of the barrel and press it down.

## 89 TRY A FULL-BORE SLUG

As long as sabot slugs cost $3 apiece, full-bore slugs selling for under $5 per box of five will always have a market. If your deer gun is a smoothbore, or if you expect to empty your magazine several times during the course of a few deer drives, or if your shots occur well under 100 yards, then full-bore slugs are for you. As an added benefit, any slug measuring .729 puts a very large hole in whatever it hits and usually comes out the other side. And full-bore slugs are much more accurate than they used to be. The best of them will shoot under 2 inches at 75 yards in a gun they like. Accuracy gets dicey after that, as the slugs slow and pass through the sound barrier between 75 and 100 yards. And they'll often group poorly and end up leaving out-of-round or even sideways holes in the target.

 **USE THE FORCE**

Like Luke Skywalker, you can use the Force to hit targets with your eyes closed. I stole this trick from instructors Gil and Vicki Ash. It's fun to try and a great way to learn what it means to have a feel for the target, as well as an excellent method for breaking yourself of the habit of looking back at the barrel to be sure (and by "to be sure" I mean "to guarantee a miss") before you shoot. If you're shooting with your eyes closed, you have to let go.

Call for the target with your eyes open. Focus on it, read its angle, and move the gun in time with the bird. Close both eyes as you start to pull the trigger. You'll crush the target. Once that becomes too easy, call for the bird and close both eyes a full second before you shoot. Stretch out, use your feelings—all that Jedi stuff—and you will be amazed at what you can do if you read the target's line and move the gun in sync with the clay.

After I showed this to two of our high school shooters who had bead-checking problems, I challenged one of them to shoot a whole round closing his eyes before pulling the trigger. He shot 22x25 and afterward admitted to opening his eyes twice during the round. He missed those two shots.

# 91 HIT FROM THE HIP

Learning to shoot clays from the hip is surprisingly easy once you learn the trick to practicing. With your gun unloaded, lay your trigger finger along the side of the receiver, so it points where the gun points.

Now, call for a few targets and pretend to shoot them. Think about pointing your trigger finger, not the gun. After years of trying and failing to shoot from the hip, it took me only a few practice points before I was able to hip shoot targets. After doing this exercise, I can hit them from the 27-yard line of the trap field . . . sometimes.

# 92 SHOOT A CHIP

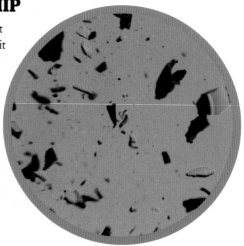

Shooting target chips is fun. It's great practice. And while it's not difficult, it impresses the easily impressed. Chip shooting works best with outgoing targets. Shoot it, look for the biggest piece, and shoot it. You will be surprised at how small a piece you can rebreak. It teaches you to "stay in the gun": to keep the gun on your face after the first shot. And, to borrow a phrase from anglers: "A clay target is too valuable to shoot only once."

# 93 HAVE FUN WITH TARGETS

For more fun at the range, you can buy the flash targets we shoot on *The Gun Nuts* TV show or make your own. Buy some snap-line chalk, put some in the dome of a target, and glue paper over the top. An easier way is to find the right size plastic drink lids to hold the chalk on the underside of the clay, but then you'll have to clean those up after you're done shooting.

You can also put a tail on a target. Use 18 inches of surveyor's tape. Fix it to the bottom of the dome with clear packing tape and roll the tail up inside the clay. When you throw it, the tail streams out behind.

Another option is to piggyback a mini. Use some rubber cement to glue a mini target inside a standard clay. When you break the larger clay, the smaller one keeps going, "like an escape pod," as someone put it.

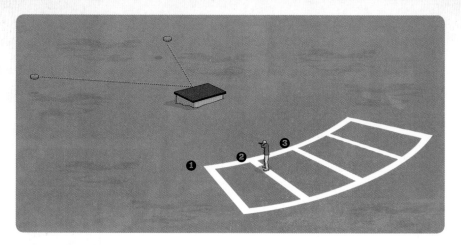

# 94 SHOOT A ROUND OF TRAP

A round of trap consists of 25 shots. You will shoot five in turn with the other shooters at each of five posts. You will need a pouch or deep pocket to hold your shells and, ideally, another pocket for your empty hulls.

Trap is shot in silence because a steady, uninterrupted rhythm helps everyone shoot their best. Load your gun as the person before you is shooting. If your semiauto ejects shells onto the ground, leave them until you change posts after five shots.

*Browning Citori Trap XT*

# 95 GET THE RIGHT TRAP GUN

Trap is a medium- to long-range game, with most targets shot at 35 yards away. Trap guns are 12 gauges with tight chokes. They have long barrels to point smoothly and are heavy to absorb recoil. Most trap guns have a high point of impact to deal with rising, going away targets. Many guns have weird, high ribs, recoil reducing stocks, and other features to help shooters deal with the repetitive pounding of hundreds of rounds in competition.

# 96 ADAPT A FIELD GUN FOR TRAP

A field gun will easily see you through many rounds of social or league trap and your first few 25 straights. Screw in a Modified, Improved Modified, or Full choke and shoot 1-ounce loads of 8 shot.

It is much easier to hit trap targets if you don't have to cover them with the barrel. Raising the comb of your field gun slightly either with shims or an aftermarket comb pad will adjust the stock to make the gun shoot higher, letting you "float" targets over the gun.

If you shoot a semiauto you will also want to be sure you have a shell catcher or at least a thick rubber band around the receiver to keep your empties from hitting the person to your right.

# 97 KNOW YOUR HOLD POINTS

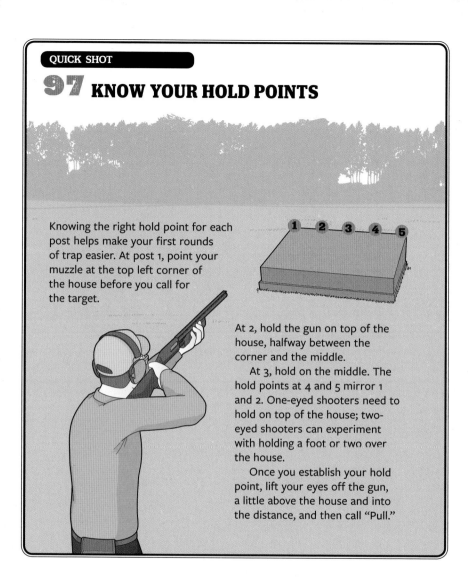

Knowing the right hold point for each post helps make your first rounds of trap easier. At post 1, point your muzzle at the top left corner of the house before you call for the target.

At 2, hold the gun on top of the house, halfway between the corner and the middle.

At 3, hold on the middle. The hold points at 4 and 5 mirror 1 and 2. One-eyed shooters need to hold on top of the house; two-eyed shooters can experiment with holding a foot or two over the house.

Once you establish your hold point, lift your eyes off the gun, a little above the house and into the distance, and then call "Pull."

# 98 SHOOT A ROUND OF SKEET

A round of skeet consists of 25 shots. Stations run in an arc from the high house to the low, with the last station, 8, located between the houses in the middle of the field. You shoot a high house and low house target at each station, and doubles at stations 1, 2, 6, and 7. You repeat your first miss, called the "option," and if you don't miss, you shoot the last shot, station 8 low, twice.

Besides following the normal rules of gun safety, be sure to wait until it's your turn to shoot and you are standing on the station—not walking up to it—before you drop shells in your gun.

# 99 CHOOSE A SKEET GUN

Skeet began as practice for grouse hunting, and a skeet field is the best place to hone all-around wingshooting skills. Any open-choked gun that shoots twice works. The short-range targets also make skeet a perfect fit for smallbores. The first 25 straight I ever shot at skeet was with a 28-gauge Browning Pump. The 28 is a great, low-recoil, hard-hitting skeet gauge, while the .410 is, let us say, "challenging."

Skeet shooters use tiny 9 shot. If you can't find it, 8s work almost as well.

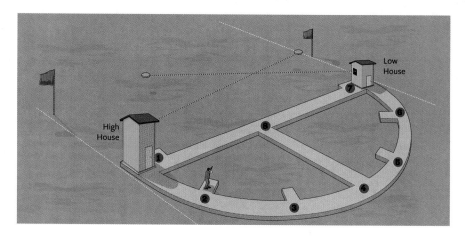

# 1⬤⬤ HIT YOUR CLAYS

Skeet targets fly on a known path when you call for them. You can set yourself up for every shot. Except for station 1 and high 8, right-handed shooters should point their belly button at the low-house window (left-handers point at the high-house window, except for 7 and low 8). Start your gun roughly one-third of the way from the house you are shooting to the center of the field. Hold it low enough that you see the target over your gun.

Skeet targets at 3, 4, and 5 require lots of lead even though they are only 20 yards away. Remember that in this case you have a 30-inch-wide pattern to put in front of the bird, so there is no need to be precise. Don't overthink it, just get the gun out in front of the target, focus on the bird, and pull the trigger.

Station 8, where the bird flies almost right at you, terrorizes beginners but is not so frightening once you know how to handle it. Start your gun at the bottom of the house window and a few feet to the side. Look into the window and concentrate on seeing the bird emerge. Shoot at the front edge, and it will turn into a black or white (depending on whether the target is pitch or biodegradable) cloud of smoke.

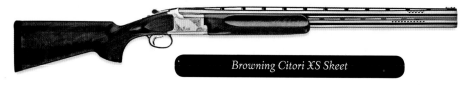

*Browning Citori XS Skeet*

# 1⬤1 KNOW YOUR OPTIONS

American skeet competitions are held in 12, 20, 28, and .410. Most competitive shooters in American skeet use one O/U with sub gauge tube sets, allowing them to shoot all four gauges with the same gun. Skeet guns have open chokes as targets are shot at close range. Most skeet guns have 28- or 30-inch barrels.

# 102 USE WHAT YOU WANT

Sporting clays guns can be anything that fires two shots. You should never be afraid to show up with your hunting gun if all you want is target practice, but among competitors, guns tend to be O/U or semiautomatic. Twelve-gauge shotguns predominate, and most guns have long barrels: 30 inches for semiautos, 30, 32, even 34 for O/Us. Extended choke tubes offer easy changes on the course. Because so many targets are shot falling, a gun that shoots fairly flat is best.

If you want to own one gun that you can use for all clay target games (and also for doves!), a dedicated sporting clays gun would be an excellent choice.

# 103 SHOOT A ROUND OF SPORTING CLAYS

A round of sporting clays consists of either 50 or 100 targets. Bring that many shells plus a few extras. Targets are shot as pairs, and you will take turns in the shooting cage shooting five pairs in succession. Never load more than two shells in your gun and do not load the gun before you're standing in the cage. The first shooter at each station can ask to see a pair of "show" targets. The shooting order rotates from one station to the next.

You will need a bag to carry your shells around the course, and you can bring chokes and change them between stations if you choose. I usually throw in a water bottle, too. Most sporting clays targets can be broken with an Improved Cylinder choke and $7^{1}/_{2}$ or 8 shot.

Sporting clays is usually much more informal and sociable than trap (especially trap) and skeet. Behavior such as congratulations, fist bumps, and friendly heckling is usually allowed.

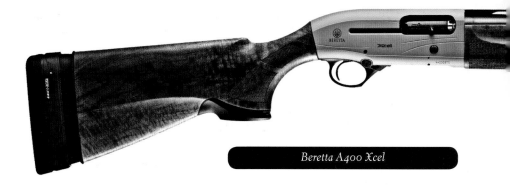

*Beretta A400 Xcel*

# 104 PLAY THE HUNTER'S GAME

"Skrap" or "upland angles" uses a combination trap/skeet field and combines the best of trap and skeet for upland hunting practice. Skeet, although invented by grouse hunters and suitable for upland guns, is best as practice for doves and waterfowl with its incoming and crossing targets. Trap has going away targets that simulate the flight of flushing upland birds, but it allows a pre-mounted gun, and dedicated trap guns don't belong out in the field.

Skrap is trap shot from the skeet stations. Rules vary, but the way I play it, you start with a low gun, get two shots at every target, and a hit with the second shot counts as much as a hit with the first shot. The puller is allowed to delay the pull by up to 3 seconds. You shoot three targets from stations 1 to 7 and four from station 8 to make a round of 25 birds. You'll have fun, and you'll be a better bird shot when the round is over.

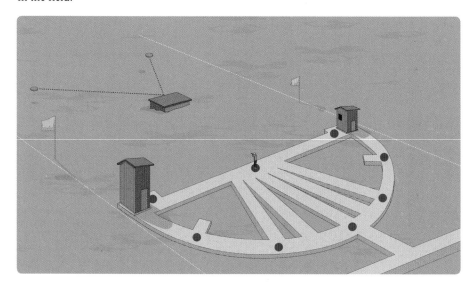

# 105 EXCEL AT SPORTING CLAYS

Sporting clays shows you all the targets you will see on the trap and skeet fields, as well as specialty targets that make the game more fun, frustrating, and challenging. And, you shoot them as pairs. Here's how.

**RABBITS** Rabbits are special hardened clays that bounce in front of the guns. The trick is to hold your muzzle below the path of the rabbit so that you can see it. Then focus hard on the target, and your eye-hand coordination will cope with any bad bounces (hint: there will always be bad bounces).

**TEAL** Teal go straight up, seem to hang for an instant, and fall. Hold your gun to one side of the flight path so you can see the bird and about a third of the way to the top of its flight. As it hangs, imagine it's a clock face, look at 6:00, and shoot.

**CHANDELLES AND BATTUES** Arcing and falling, chandelles and battues require lead both in front and below. Using the clock face analogy again, look at 5:00 on the right-hand targets, 7:00 on the left, and give them more lead in front than you think they need.

# 106 CHOOSE YOUR SKRAP GUN

Shots in skrap are long, with the exception of station 8. If your bird gun has choke tubes, go with Modified and Full from stations 1 to 7 and switch to Skeet or Improved Cylinder for the last four birds. Any gun of any gauge goes, but even in a clay game like this that attempts to simulate bird hunting, a dedicated sporting clays gun will win.

# 107 TRY THE SMALLBORE VERSION

You can modify skrap to make it more smallbore-friendly and to better simulate typical upland shots by setting the stations closer to the house. Our local Ruffed Grouse Society chapter used to hold a fun shoot/competition and encouraged hunters to bring their open-choked, small-gauge grouse guns. They marked stations on the course with hula hoops (shooters have to have at least one foot in the hoop) 7 to 12 yards behind the house, with stations 1 and 7 directly on either side of the trap, and station 8 immediately behind it.

# 108 USE A SHOTGUN FOR DEFENSE

Despite what you see in the movies, buckshot can't knock down walls or send people flying through the air. Nevertheless, shotguns make devastating close-range defense weapons. According to a recent Harris/National Shooting Sports Foundation poll, "home protection" is the leading reason Americans purchased their most recent firearm, so it's not surprising that Federal, Remington, and Winchester have developed new home-defense loads ranging from birdshot in .410 to 00 buck over a slug in 12 gauge.

What makes a "home defense" load? Loads designed for indoor use have to pattern openly to hit a close-range target. They have to stop, incapacitate, or dissuade an attacker; ideally, pellets that don't hit the target won't pass through several walls to harm family members and neighbors. Most home-defense shootings occur at a range of 5 to 7 yards, so to test home-defense loads, I did my patterning at that distance, with a few longer 10- to 15-yard shots thrown in. Here's what I ended up learning.

**IT ALL GOES THROUGH WALLS** Birdshot easily penetrates two thicknesses of wallboard; buckshot can cut through half a dozen. Years ago I blasted a hole through the side of a chicken house with No. 7 ½ shot while trying to defend our flock from a weasel.

**RIFLING AND BUCKSHOT DON'T MIX** Rifling spins pellets in an expanding donut pattern. At seven steps, every single pellet of a 00 buck load missed a 14x16-inch target—twice—from my Deerslayer.

**SHOTGUNS ARE NOT AREA WEAPONS** At typical five-to-seven-step home-defense range, even an open choke throws a pattern only 6 or 7 inches wide. That said, the advantage of shot over bullets is margin for aiming error. A 6-inch pattern 7 inches off center will still put some pellets into the vital zone.

**PATTERN YOUR SHOTGUN** An unchoked sawed-off shotgun is supposed to spray the widest patterns of all. Rather than put a hacksaw to my Benelli, I screwed in a pure Cylinder tube and tried both Federal 4 buck and a hunting load of 000 buck. Surprisingly, the Cylinder shot tight 3-inch clumps at 5 yards with each. With an Improved Cylinder choke, the patterns opened up to 6 inches. Based on my results, I would recommend Skeet or IC chokes. But before you trust your life to it, shouldn't you find out how it will shoot?

# 109 DON'T DON'T STOP YOUR SWING

"Don't stop your swing" is the most common and the worst advice you'll hear at the gun club. It addresses a symptom (stopping the gun) not the cause (looking at the gun). People take it to heart and add a lurching follow-through to their swing-stop-shoot sequence that doesn't change a thing.

# 110 TEACH EACH OTHER

You and a friend can help each other learn to shoot better with only a hand trap and a few boxes of clays, if you learn how to teach. Telling someone where he or she missed doesn't help; you have to tell them why. The key is to watch the shooter's muzzle. The muzzle goes where the eyes send it. With a little practice, you can practically read a shooter's mind by watching where the gun goes.

If someone's gun stops short, it is not because the shooter consciously stopped his swing, it's because he looked from the target to the barrels to measure lead or to double-check. When the muzzles pop over the top of a going away bird, it usually means the shooter didn't focus his eyes on the target hard enough. Missing high and behind a crossing or quartering target often means the shooter had the gun too high, and it actually blocked his view of the target for an instant.

Watch for head lifting, too, which is the other main cause of missing high.

# 111 READ A GOLF BOOK

There are only a couple of good books I know of about the how-to of shooting a shotgun. The *Orvis Wing-Shooting Handbook* teaches sound field style. Gil and Vicki Ash's *You've Got to Be Out of Your Mind* is an entertaining, useful look at the mental side of shooting. After you read those two, then what? Go to the golf section of your bookstore.

You'll find a long shelf of self-help golf books with touchy-feely titles like *The Inner Game of Golf, Fearless Golf, The Golf of Your Dreams, Mind Over Golf,* and *Deepak Chopra's Golf for Enlightenment.* Don't laugh. What these books teach you about the mental game of golf will help you become a better shotgunner.

Dr. Joe Parent, author of the excellent *Zen Putting* and *Zen Golf,* hasn't shot a gun himself since he was a Boy Scout, but he told me, "I coached a trapshooter for a year once. In 2003, she was browsing in a bookstore and found my book. We began consulting by phone. I helped her break her first 200 straight."

# 113 FILM YOURSELF

One of the surprise benefits of being on *The Gun Nuts* TV show has been the opportunity to see and correct mistakes in my shooting that I otherwise would never have noticed. For instance, I sometimes pull the gun off my face when I shoot right to left crossers.

You can achieve the same benefit by having someone film you with a video camera, or even your phone. You'll be surprised at what you learn, and it can only help you to improve.

# 114

## LEARN TO JUMP SHOOT DUCKS

When you jump shoot ducks, you get going away shots similar to the kind upland hunters take all the time. Trap, with its rising, going away targets at unknown angles, is great practice for jump shooting. You'll want to practice this with a 16-yard trap shot, from any station.

Start with an unmounted gun, as you would in the field. Call "Pull!" and take an instant to read the angle before you move the gun. Flushing ducks often take you by surprise, and learning not to move the gun until you know where it needs to go helps you avoid rushed, futile shots. See the target and then swing the gun through it and pull the trigger. Follow through by keeping your face on the stock and your eye on the target until after it breaks.

# 115

## PRACTICE FOR FLARING BIRDS

Often your second shot in duck hunting is at birds flaring straight up out of the decoys. They appear to be hanging, but they're actually going back and up.

The practice clay you want to use for this is springing teal. Targets are launched straight up, rocketing into the air in a way no game bird actually flies. Nevertheless, they make excellent practice if you shoot them as they near the top of their flight but are still on the way up. Hold your gun to one side of the flight path to get a clear look at the bird and then jab the muzzle over the bird's head, blotting it from view. Trust that you're on target and pull the trigger right away. Imagine trying to shoot the top of the target, just as you would think about trying to scalp a jumping mallard.

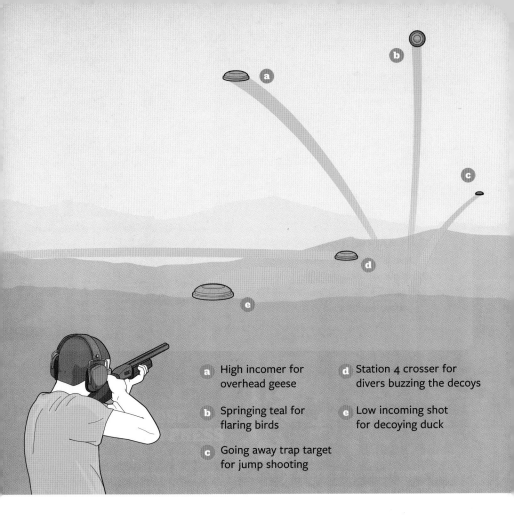

**a** High incomer for overhead geese

**b** Springing teal for flaring birds

**c** Going away trap target for jump shooting

**d** Station 4 crosser for divers buzzing the decoys

**e** Low incoming shot for decoying duck

# 116 DEAL WHEN DIVERS BUZZ THE DECOYS

Diving ducks often streak by the edge of the decoys without putting on the brakes. Station 4, in the middle of the skeet field, requires the longest leads, up to 4 feet, and makes great practice.

When you set up for a station 4 crosser, hold your gun halfway between the house and the middle of the field, and make sure it's below the target's line of flight. As the bird comes out, keep all your focus on the target, move the gun ahead of it while matching its speed, and shoot the instant you think the lead is right. For right-handed shooters, the high-house (left) target presents the temptation to pull the gun off your face. The low-house (right-hand) bird can be difficult, because they come out of the house low and get behind the gun and out of sight of a right-hander. When people miss 4, it's usually thanks to insufficient lead, or, more often, from shooters looking at the gun to double-check or measure lead.

# 117

## MAKE THE FIVE TOUGHEST SHOTS

As a nation of dove hunters, we average 5 to 8 shots for every bird bagged. With the price of shotshells, I can't afford to miss that much. I'm hoping to hit one out of three when the season starts; that's a good average if you try everything that comes into range. Although doves zipping randomly around a field present a wide variety of shots, most of those shots fall into the following five main categories.

**Dove with the Jets On** When you're in a crowded field, sometimes you have to root for a dove to get past other people so you can shoot it yourself. Problem is, when that bird reaches you, it's moving at top speed and juking all over the sky. This one is a no-brain reaction shot—you have to trust your hand-eye coordination and get your conscious mind out of the way. I like an aggressive swing-through system for these birds, which can duck out from under a maintained lead-style swing. Sweep the gun past the target from behind and shoot when the muzzle clears the beak. Because you are swinging the gun very quickly, you won't have to see much lead; just shoot as the gun clears the beak. Keep a tight focus on the target, and your eyes will magically send your hands to the right place if the dove pulls last-minute evasive maneuvers.

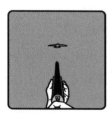

**The Incomer You See Forever** The bird that comes all the way across the field to you is surprisingly easy to screw up. It's even worse if you announce to the person next to you: "I'm going to shoot this dove." (I've done this.) Avoid the temptation to mount the gun early and track this bird all the way in. Inevitably, you'll look back at the bead to check your lead and stop the gun, or the dove will dip down below the muzzle, and you'll have to scramble to find it again. Instead, wait for it with the gun ready, butt tucked loosely under your arm. As the bird comes into range, look at the beak, make a smooth gun mount, and shoot the bird in the nostrils. This is not a fast-draw contest between you and the bird; mount the gun in time with the target's speed, keep a sharp eye on the beak, and pull the trigger when the gun meets your shoulder.

**The Surprise Dove** The bird that flies overhead from behind takes you by surprise and requires a little lead underneath. If you're a skeet shooter, you've made this shot a million times at high house 1. If not, here's what to do: Resist the temptation to rush this shot. Before you start your mount, raise the muzzle, keeping it just to the right of the bird (if you're right-handed); that way, you won't lose sight of the bird behind the gun. Move the muzzle down through the bird while raising the stock to your face. Shoot when you see the dove above your barrel. Don't shoot right at this bird; instead, try to miss it underneath, or think "graze its belly" with your pellets.

   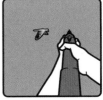

**The Long Crosser** The dove that loafs along unalarmed, crossing at 35 yards, takes a lot of forward allowance. Keep your eye on the dove and mount the muzzle in front of the bird. Swing, matching the dove's speed. Trust your subconscious mind to tell you the instant the lead is right. If you try to measure the lead, analyze it, or double-check it, your gun will either slow down or stop. You'll miss. Remember, lead doesn't have to be precise—you've got a wide pattern on your side. Focus on the bird, let the blur of the muzzle drift ahead of it, and shoot.

**The High Overhead Dove** Birds coming into a field over the treetops look impossibly high. In reality, they aren't as far up as they appear; it's a very tall oak or pine that measures 90 feet. That 30- to 35-yard shot is well within the capability of even an Improved Cylinder choke, and most trees are much shorter. And remember: A dove straight overhead is presenting all of its vitals to your shot. The higher the bird, the slower you have to move your gun. Start with the muzzle behind the bird as you raise the stock to your face and swing through the target. Keep your back leg straight with your weight on your back foot. When you can't see the dove behind the muzzle, consciously keep the gun moving and shoot. The dove will fall apparently from the stratosphere. I love this shot because it's much easier than it looks to impressed bystanders.

# INDEX

# ABOUT THE AUTHOR

**PHIL BOURJAILY** sold his first outdoor story—on snipe hunting—to *Field & Stream* in 1985. Today, he is the magazine's Shotguns columnist and co-writer, with David Petzal, of "The Gun Nuts" blog on fieldandstream.com. He is the author of the *Field & Stream Turkey Hunting Handbook* and, as a turkey hunter, has renounced early mornings in favor of sleeping in and killing spring gobblers between the hours of 9 AM and 2 PM. A 1981 graduate of the University of Virginia, he makes his home today, with his wife and two sons, in his birthplace of Iowa City, Iowa. He has traveled widely in pursuit of upland birds, waterfowl, and turkeys, but his favorite hunts are for pheasants close to home with his German shorthaired pointer, Jed.

# THANKS

Rob James and Mariah Bear of Weldon Owen held my hand every step of the way during this project, as did Dave Hurteau of *Field & Stream*. I would not be half of The Gun Nuts had Dave Petzal not made the blog a success before I joined it, and I would not be shotgun editor of *Field & Stream* had Deputy Editor Slaton White not taken an interest in a pheasant hunter from Iowa 20 years ago.

Thanks to everyone at *Field & Stream*, especially Editor-in-Chief Anthony Licata, Senior Editor Mike Toth, and Online Editor Dave Maccar. Finally, I'd like to give special thanks for the help and support of my wife Pam.

# CREDITS

**Cover images** Front and back photos: *Shutterstock*
Back illustrations: Left, *Hayden Foell* Center, *Lauren Towner* Right, *Conor Buckley*

**Photography courtesy of** *Rick Adair:* 3, 23 *Alamy:* 47 *Benelli:* 19 (10) *Beretta:* 19 (8, 11), 106 *Blue Book Publications:* 20 *Browning:* 12 (gun), 95, 101 *Jamie Chung:* 45 (shell bottoms) *Steve Doyle Portraitefx/Armsbid:* 19 (3, 5, 6, 12) *Bryce Duffy:* 79 *Federal Premium:* 31, 41 *Nick Ferrarri:* 96 *Gorman & Gorman:* 89 *Gunslick:* 61 (metal brush, soft brush) *iStock:* 55, 58, 93 *James D. Julia:* 19 (9, 13) *Krieghoff:* 19 (14), 24, 108 (gun) *Outers:* 66 (rods) *Public Domain:* 30 *Purdey:* 19 (1) *Remington:* 6, 19 (2, 4), 53, 85 *Dan Saelinger:* 5, 25 *Safariland Commercial,*

*Firearms Accessories, Hatch, Monadnock and Training Group:* 66 (Breakfree) *Shutterstock:* Title Page, 2, 10, 14 (dragonfly), 14, 16, 17, 29 (turkey), 34, 35, 36, 37, 38 (silhouettes), 39, 40, 42, 45 (shotshells), 46, 48, 50, 51, 54, 59, 61 (steel wool), 64, 66 (multitool), 71, 72, 78, 84, 90, 99, 105, 108 (figure in doorway), 109, 111, 113, 114, Index page 1, Index page 2, About the Author, Acknowledgements, Credits, Imprint, Last Page *Thompson Center Arms:* 29 (gun) *Westley Richards:* 19 (7) *Windigo Images:* 20 (men examining gun), 57, 62, 92

**Illustrations courtesy of** *Conor Buckley:* 28, 32, 46, 49, 91, 116 *Hayden Foell:* 68, 74, 77, 81, 82, 87, 94, 100, 104 *Flyingchilli.com:* 117 *Raymond Larrett:* 9, 76 *Chris Philpot:* 97 *Robert L. Prince:* 4 *Lauren Towner:* 70, 73

# FIELD & STREAM

**Editor** Anthony Licata
**VP, Group Publisher** Eric Zinczenko

2 Park Avenue
New York, NY 10016
www.fieldandstream.com

# weldon**owen**

**President, CEO** Terry Newell
**VP, Publisher** Roger Shaw
**Executive Editor** Mariah Bear
**Editorial Assistant** Ian Cannon
**Creative Director** Kelly Booth
**Art Director** Barbara Genetin
**Designer** Michel Gadwa
**Cover Design** William Mack
**Illustration Coordinator** Conor Buckley
**Production Director** Chris Hemesath
**Production Manager** Michelle Duggan

All of the material in this book was originally
published in *The Total Gun Manual*, by David E.
Petzal and Phil Bourjaily.

Weldon Owen would like to thank William Mack for
the original design concept adapted from *The Total Gun
Manual*. Marisa Solis provided editorial assistance.

© 2012 Weldon Owen Inc.

415 Jackson Street
San Francisco, CA 94111
www.weldonowen.com

*Field & Stream* and Weldon Owen are divisions of
# BONNIER

Library of Congress Control Number on file with the
publisher

ISBN 13: 978-1-61628-485-5
ISBN 10: 1-61628-485-4

10 9 8 7 6 5 4 3 2 1

2012 2013 2014 2015

Printed in China by 1010